THE EXPERIENTIAL DIMENSION OF ADVAITA VEDANTA

THE EXPERIENTIAL DIMENSION OF

Advaita Vedanta

ARVIND SHARMA

MOTILAL BANARSIDASS PUBLISHERS
PRIVATE LIMITED • DELHI

First Edition : Delhi, 1993

ISBN: 81-208-1058-9

Also available at:
MOTILAL BANARSIDASS
41 U.A. Bungalow Road, Jawahar Nagar, Delhi 110 007
120 Royapettah High Road, Mylapore, Madras 600 004
16 St. Mark's Road, Bangalore 560 001
Ashok Rajpath, Patna 800 004
Chowk, Varanasi 221 001

PRINTED IN INDIA

BY JAINENDRA PRAKASH JAIN AT SHRI JAINENDRA PRESS,
A-45 NARAINA INDUSTRIAL AREA, PHASE I, NEW DELHI 110 028
AND PUBLISHED BY NARENDRA PRAKASH JAIN FOR MOTILAL
BANARSIDASS PUBLISHERS PVT. LTD., BUNGALOW ROAD,
JAWAHAR NAGAR, DELHI 110 007

For

Eliot Deutsch

The truth is NEITHER one nor two. It is as it is.[1]

Ramana

Each man's first duty is to realize his true nature. If after doing this he feels like reforming the country or nation, by all means let him take up such reform.[2]

Ramana

Gold is not an ornament but an ornament is nothing but gold.[3]

Ramana

I am' is the ultimate fact; 'Who am I?' is the ultimate question to which everybody must find an answer.[4]

Nisargadatta

CONTENTS

PREFACE

This book is intended for those who have either a fleeting or nodding acquaintance with Hindu thought or a curiosity about it, specially that part of it known as Advaita *Vedanta*, but have also wondered whether this body of thought has anything to do with the daily experience of living. This book makes the claim that—stripped bare of the Sanskrit language and the cultural idiom in which it is expressed—this body of thought offers an analysis of life which bears a direct relevance to our daily business of living. The relevance is in fact so direct that no Sanskrit word other than *Advaita* itself may be required in expounding it, and no authority at all need be invoked in elaborating it except that of experience; the experience of those of whom it may be claimed that they have actually undergone the experience which the body of thought seeks to explore. In the pages of this book the reader will encounter only five major terms or names with which the reader may not already be familiar: Advaita Vedanta (Advaita for short); Sankara, Ramana and Nisargadatta.

The word *Vedanta* refers to a body of texts which form the concluding section of the Hindu scripture known as the Veda, just as the Revelation of St. John constitutes the concluding section of the Bible. *Advaita* Vedanta indicates one of the many systematic philosophical expositions which these texts have generated within Hinduism. This particular exposition, developed by the exegete Sankara—(788-820), upholds the conclusion that in the final analysis the ultimate reality about the universe is a unity entirely indivisible and hence non-dual: this is the meaning of the word *Advaita*. This non-dual reality can be directly experienced.

Ramana (1879-1950) and Nisargadatta (1897-1981) are two figures of modern India about whom it has been claimed that an encounter with this reality made an "experienceable difference" to their lives. While Ramana is too well known to need an introduction, the life of Nisargadatta may be presented in brief, as follows:

> Sri Nisargadatta Maharaj was born in Bombay in 1897. His parents, who gave him the name Maruti, had a small farm at the village of Kandalgaon and it was here that he spent his early years. In 1924 he married, later becoming a cigarette trader in Bombay where he and his wife raised a family. From early childhood he had taken a keen interest in spiritual matters, his talks with holy men sharpening his inquisitive mind and kindling a spiritual fire. At the age of 34 he met his Guru and three years later realized himself, taking the name of Nisargadatta. He continued to live the life of an ordinary Indian working-man but his teachings, which he set out in his master-work I Am That and which are rooted in the ancient Upanishadic tradition, made a significant philosophical break from contemporary thought. Devotees travelled from all over the world to hear Nisargadatta's unique message until his death in 1981.[5]

INTRODUCTION

The *doctrinal* philosophy of Advaita is characterized by the affirmation of the existence of a "sole spiritual reality".[6] One may well ask:

> What is the bearing of such a view of ultimate reality on our everyday life? The most striking feature of the latter is the conviction which it involves, viz. that diversity is real and ultimate. The presupposition of most, if not all, of the activities of life is that one man is different from another. The very efforts made through social and political organizations to unify men imply that they regard themselves as distinct. If man is distinct from man, his distinction from his physical environment is even clearer. It is not merely man that is distinct from matter; matter itself, whether it serves as an adjunct of the self like the physical body and the organs of sense or as its environment, seems to be diverse in its character, each object having its own individuality .... It is obvious that, if monism is the truth, no part of this diversity can be ultimate. That is the significance of the teaching .... so far as our common beliefs are concerned.[7]

A little reflection will show that the significance of the teaching is even more radical. For if there is only *one* reality, *we* must be *identical* with it! When Advaita is faced with the logical necessity as well as the apparent implausibility of such a conclusion it appeals to a life-transforming experience which enables one "to grasp the unity of experience directly—as directly as he has grasped its diversity," on the principle "that a mediate knowledge of truth cannot overcome an immediate illusion—that seeing alone is believing."[8]

There is our ordinary experience of daily living. Advaita intrudes into it with the claim that an extraordinary experience is possible in this life which can cause a Copernican revolution within it. This transformation of ordinary experience by the Advaitin experience represents a claim so astounding that on this basis alone it needs at least to be examined. But has anyone undergone such an experience to make it accessible to investigation? Most Advaitins are agreed that the modern Hindu sage Ramana (1879-1950) had undergone it. This view is shared by Nisargadatta (1897-1981) about whom a similar claim has also been made. Thus Ramana may be said to be the chief spokesman of *experiential* Advaita just as the philosopher Sankara (788-820) is looked upon as the leading expositor of *doctrinal* Advaita.

This book attempts an exploration of experiential Advaita. Any such exploration must (1) begin with a statement about the nature of ordinary or normal experience; (2) subject it to a suitable critique; (3) if the critique is plausible, reformulate ordinary experience in the light of this critique and, finally (4) compare its own putative experience of (ultimate) reality with our daily experience of ordinary reality. Thus are the four chapters of the first part of the book accounted for. The second part explores these issues further.

The term *experience* is an ambiguous one. It may refer to the experience of ordinary people like you and me or of extraordinary people like Ramana and Nisargadatta. It may also refer not only to the ordinary experiences of ordinary people and the extraordinary experiences of extraordinary people but to the extraordinary experiences of ordinary people and the ordinary experiences of extraordinary people. Thus the discussion of experience raises two questions: *who's experience* and *which experience*? Ambiguity is usually viewed negatively, but in the present context could it not turn into something creative?

PART I

CHAPTER I

WHAT IS NORMAL EXPERIENCE ?

I

There are three conclusions which become immediately obvious even on a perfunctory review of our everyday life: (1) that human beings exist; (2) that all normal human beings experience the states of waking, dreaming and dreamless sleep in the normal course of living and that (3) out of these three states, they accord primacy to the waking state.

The fundamental claim of experiential or existential Advaita is precisely this, that "one can discover the nature of existence by analyzing one's own existence as manifest in experience."[9] Moreover, while the "state of waking has a vantage-point . . . inquiry should not be restricted to the implications of waking state alone, for waking is only a segment of experience . . . inquiry in order to be fruitful must take into account the total experience. It is thus that the inquiry into the three states becomes supremely important..."[10]

II

It is obvious that not only do all *normal* human beings experience the states of waking, dreaming and deep sleep but that all that is experienced by human beings *normally* occurs in these states. That normal human beings experience waking, dreaming and dreamless sleep is obvious; we do occasionally read accounts of people who haven't slept for years but this is clearly accepted as abnormal. It may again be the case that some human beings may not dream for long periods of time—either in terms of the duration of dreams or the intervals between them—but here again it is often the case that the dreams did occur but have been more or less immediately forgotten. Similarly, there are *transitional* states such as the hypnogogic (preceding sleep) and hypnopompic (preceding awakening), and *abnormal* states such as those of fainting, coma, etc. which may be at least temporarily excluded from consideration as we wish to focus on normal experience. It would seem fair to say, then, that normal experience is comprised of three states: waking, dreaming and dreamless sleep.

That out of these three states the waking is supposed to be the primary, indeed the only "real" one, is also apparent. On a popular view, in dreaming the brain processes the information received in the waking state and in deep sleep the body and mind rest and recover to engage in the activity of living in the waking state once again. These facts are so patent and obvious that one tends to overlook them.

Advaita takes these facts of daily living as the starting point of its investigation. There is widespread acknowledgement of the primacy accorded to the waking state in both doctrinal and experiential Advaita. Thus Ramana clearly states that for the average person of the world *"the standard of reality is the waking state,"*[11] and this obvious fact is often reflected in works on Advaita:

> Ordinarily, we consider our lives to be taken up with our waking condition. We do not attach any importance to sleep and dream states. They are reckoned as durations lost to the sum total of our lives. Western psychology deals mostly with the waking state and incidentally with dreams as explaining the abnormalities of waking life.[12]

In this respect the Advaitin perspective represents a pivotal shift. It may even be said that Advaita "owes its significance to its unique attitude towards life, which it views from an angle of vision altogether its own. While others concentrate their attention on the world before us, which is taken to comprehend all the reality that we can know, and while sleep and dream-experiences are utilized to explain the phenomena of waking life,"[13] Advaita "proposes to deal with life as it manifests itself in all the three states and so determines the nature of reality as a whole. The two viewpoints differ fundamentally. In the one, the waking world represents all our real interests, and sleep and dream are gently put aside as mere appendages of waking. But in the other, each of the states is given a right place and is invested with equal significance."[14]

Before one turns to an examination of the Advaitin position in this connection, it would be helpful to ask and try to answer the following question: Why is it that ordinarily human beings tend to accord primacy to the state of waking over those of dream and dreamless sleep to such an extent that they regard it as the yardstick for judging the other two, and even regard the other two as less consequential or even less real than the waking state, when in fact all three states are experienced?

The following reasons may be listed in support of the everyday assumption that it is the waking state in which we are truly alive.

(1) It is estimated that human beings spend about a third of their life in "sleep"—which would include both dreaming and dreamless sleep. Judged by this quantitative criterion, obviously more of our life is "lived" in the waking than in any other state and it must therefore be accorded priority, as it is of longer duration than the other two.

(2) The waking state is more real than dreaming and dreamless sleep because while we can recollect in the waking state that we slept and/or dreamt the reverse is not true.

(3) In relation to the dream state in particular, the waking state may be said to be more objective in the following ways:

(i) In the waking state the physical objects experienced by us are distinct from us and outside us; whereas in a dream even though objects may be experienced as distinct from us they are not outside us;

(ii) Upon waking from a dream we return to the same waking world but on going back to dreaming we do not return to the same dream, except in exceptional cases of recurrent nightmares;

(iii) Dreams are of the nature of illusion and "the dream world lacks the slightest empirical reality precisely because the spatial, temporal and causal relations known in a dream are contradicted and sublated upon waking."[15] Moreover, dream objects are not real. The food I dreamt about cannot satisfy my hunger in the waking state.

(iv) Dreams are self-contradictory in a way that the waking state is not, though it is characterized by change, for "one event in a dream is also cancelled by another. What appears as a chariot turns suddenly into a man, and the man again turns into a tree."[16]

(v) A dream is a private experience. While a table seen in a dream is in *one individual's* mind, experiences in the waking state, at least of external objects, are public and verifiable: *many individuals* see the same table.

(vi) A contradicting experience is superior to a contradicted experience, as the experience of a rope which contradicts the earlier experience of mistaking the rope for a snake. Similarly, the contradicting experience of the waking state is superior to the contradicted experience of a dream.

(vii) The waking state is more real than the dream state because in one cycle of waking-dreaming-deep sleep, the waking state is of longer duration. For such reasons even a philosopher who may be a "staunch advocate of the greater creativity of dream consciousness" has to admit that:

> Dreams do not deny the truth of waking life as a whole . . . Waking, however, denies the truth of dreams.[17]

(4) In relation to dreamless sleep, the waking state is more real because it is characterized by experiences. Dreams are also characterized by experiences but it was demonstrated earlier how waking state experiences are more real than dream experiences.

(5) The physical body persists through the states of waking, dream and dreamless sleep, although body-consciousness is absent in the last two states. But as we are conscious of the body only in the waking state it obviously is more real compared to the other two.

(6) In the states of dreamless sleep and dream we are devoid of any memory of the contents of the waking state (although experiences undergone in the waking state may influence experiences in these states). On the other hand one possesses a clear memory of the contents of the two other states in the waking state (even if not in full).

(7) Perception is a greater reality in the waking state than in either dream or dreamless sleep. It is distorted in the former and absent in the latter.

(8) Suffering is more real in the waking state than in dream or dreamless sleep. It is absent in dreamless sleep. It may be present in dreams but one does not *return* to it on dreaming again the way one returns to the same suffering again on waking up.

(9) Waking is more real than dreaming and deep sleep because it provides the basis for them both. Thus the contents of dreams are often drawn from the waking state and exhaustion in the waking state leads to deep sleep.

(10) The most significant argument in favour of assigning to the waking state the pride of place among all states seems to be that in this state the *maximum exercise of volition* is possible.

(11) By contrast, sleep represents a state of simple unconsciousness—not merely one in which no conscious effort can be made, but one in which the sleeper is devoid of all consciousness itself. In this sense deep sleep is inferior to both waking and dreaming.

CHAPTER II

A CRITIQUE OF NORMAL EXPERIENCE

Advaita provides counterarguments to these points from its own perspective. These arguments do not constitute the *proof* of the Advaitin position which can only come from direct experience of a kind which will be discussed later. But these counterarguments do serve to establish the *plausibility* of the Advaitin position.

(1) Mere quantity is a poor test of the importance of a state; the concept of quality must also be brought into play. It may be that most of life is spent in the waking state in terms of quantity-time but it is quality-time which really counts. For instance, when one is asked to recall the high points of a year, these may in all only constitute a few months, weeks, days or even minutes of it but make the entire year significant and memorable.

(2) Although we recall having dreamt when in the waking state and not vice versa it is clear that the dream state sometimes influences waking—as in wet dreams. Moreover, while we can

recall dreams in waking; dreams have the power to wake us up or call us up into waking, as through a nightmare. Again, although I may not be able to recall the dream, it is clear that I, the waking person, was present in both dream and deep sleep because when I wake up I regard myself as the same person who dreamt and slept; hence I must have been present. If one asks: "Why is it that we remember dreams when awake but not the reverse"? one might answer "You are wrong. You are yourself in the dream and identify yourself as the one now speaking!"[18] Moreover, "every one will recollect strange perplexities in the dream. One wonders if he dreams or is awake. He argues and determines that he is only awake. When really awake he finds that all that was only a dream."[19]

It appears, on closer scrutiny, that two answers are offered by experiential Advaita to the question: Why do we remember dreams in the waking state and not vice versa? We remember dreams in the waking state because the dreams represent an intrusion into sleep of the mental impressions of the waking state, hence they are recalled in the waking state.[20] Dreams do not constitute an intrusion into the waking state, hence we do not recall the waking state in dreams. The incursion of dream into waking is in the form of an event in the waking state, hence again dreams are remembered in the waking state and not vice versa. Thus so far as the *fact* of existence is concerned there is continuity between dreaming and waking. Inasmuch as the purpose of the comment 'we recollect our dreams when awake and not vice versa' is to establish continuity between waking and dreaming from the waking point of view and question it from the dreaming point of view, Advaita asserts such continuity by claiming: "You are yourself in the dream and identify yourself as the one now speaking."[21] If it be argued that this fact is known only in the waking state the Advaitin conclusion is that therefore "realization can only take place in the waking state!"[22] It should be noted however that it is not strictly true that in the dream we are entirely unaware of waking for "*in the dream*—you identify yourself with the one now speaking."[23]

Another argument seems possible; that as in "waking state, ego identifies itself with the physical body and in dream with the subtle mind,"[24] the gross can recall the subtle but the subtle cannot recall the gross.

Furthermore, it could be said that the fact that we can recall dreaming in the waking state suggests the possibility that the waking state could be like a dream, whereas to recall the waking state in a dream would serve no such purpose.

A more profound metaphysical point is also involved. From one point of view, in normal existence "one is always in sleep only. The present waking state is no more than a dream. Dream can take place only in sleep. Sleep is underlying these three states. The display of those three states is again a dream which in its turn, is another sleep."[25] Thus there is really no waking up in which we can say that now we are awake whereas earlier we dreamt. So the question really is: if the waking state equals Dream I and the dreaming state equals Dream II, why can we recall Dream II in Dream I and not Dream I in Dream II? The answer: because Dream I is *longer* in duration than Dream II and hence can't be recalled in Dream II. This seems to be one implication of Ramana's answers to the question: Is there any genuine difference between dream experience and the waking state? Ramana feels that there is really none; it only appears to exist: "Because we find the dream creations transitory in relation to the waking state, there is said to be a difference."[26] Elsewhere he says: "There is no difference between dream and the waking state except that the dream is *short* and the waking *long.*"[27] The short is recalled in the long, not the long in the short. One can experience and recall how ten minutes passed within the hour, but the hour cannot be experienced and recalled in ten minutes.

(3) The various points indicating the waking state's greater objectivity may now be discussed.

(i) There are several responses to this from the point of view of experiential Advaita. (a) "It may be said that in a dream there is no actual physical object which we cognize; but in waking life there is a physical object. How do you know that there is a table or a ball in waking life? Your information is by the interpretation of sense impressions. You have the same kind of sense impressions in a dream. The feeling that there is an object external to oneself is common both to waking and to dream life."[28] (b) The objects in the dream are seen as outside us only *after* the dream is over. Is it not then possible that although objects appear distinct to us in the waking state, it may be so only *while* we are awake? The mind "cannot deny the reality of the dream world while it is dreaming and it cannot deny the reality of the waking world while it is awake."[29]

(ii) (a) To begin with, we do *not* return to the same world but to a similar world upon waking from a dream. It seems to be the same world "on account of wrong ideas. When someone says that he took a bath in the same river twice he is wrong, because when he bathed for the second time the river was not the same as it was when he bathed for the first time. On looking twice at the brightness of a flame a man says that he sees the same flame, but this flame is changing every moment. The waking state is like this. The stationary appearance is an error of perception."[30]

(b) Nevertheless one does return to a similar world in a sense which one does not in a dream. This is because there is one crucial difference between the waking state and the dream state. In the waking state the physical body is invariably experienced as present in the world while this is not so in dreams. We can see objects in a dream without being present in the dream as such.

(iii) Ramana responds to this point as follows: "All this talk about inconsistencies in the dream-world arises only now, when you are awake. While you are dreaming, the dream was a perfectly integrated whole. That is to say, if you felt thirsty in a dream, the illusory drinking of illusory water quenched your illusory thirst. But all this was real and not illusory to you so long as you did not know that the dream itself was illusory. Similarly with the waking world. The sensations you now have get co-ordinated to give you the impression that the world is real."[31]

The point can be pressed even further. It can, of course, be said: "But dream objects are not real. Water in a dream will not quench your thirst, money seen in it cannot make you rich. Here again is a misapplication of standards. Dream-water can quench dream-thirst and the dream-money can convert the dreaming pauper into a rich man during the dream. *Per contra, waking life water cannot quench dream thirst, nor can money in his box make the dreaming 'pauper' feel that he is rich. Each is false by the standard of the other.*"[32]

It could therefore be plausibly argued that the truth of the matter is as follows: "When you identify yourself with the body as in . . . (waking state) you see gross objects; when in subtle body or in the mental plane as in dream you see objects equally subtle; in the absence of identification as in sleep you see nothing. The objects seen bear a relationship to the state of the seer."[33]

(iv) The counterargument here is the one cited earlier, that "all this talk about inconsistencies in the dream-world arises only now, when you are awake. While you are dreaming, the dream was a perfectly integrated whole."[34] Moreover, is the waking state free from inconsistencies? For instance, in the waking state "the validity of sense perception is not fully established," because in some cases it is cancelled by itself, as when we realize we mistook someone or something for someone or something else. Thus a rope may be mistaken for a snake and then recognized as a rope. Moreover, inference contradicts perception occasionally as in the case of "the perception from below of cows grazing on a mountain as very small."[35] Again, we say we travelled by ship from, for example, New York to London. But what is the fact? It was the *ship* that moved, one just sat in it. "Even from the ordinary point of view you sit in the cabin and the ship sails but you do not move."[36]

(v) This is a fairly common and apparently strong argument until it is noted that "in dreams too many people appear; they talk to each other and to the dreamer,"[37] and may see and even operate objects in common. Thus "a community of experiences among the waking people" is not confined to the waking state and extends to dreams. Moreover, "just as you seek corroboration about waking state experiences from those whom you meet in the waking state, so you have to ask for corroboration about the dream experiences from those whom you meet in the dream state."[38]

(vi) It may be admitted that a contradicting experience is superior to a contradicted experience, and waking contradicts the dream state. However dreams also contradict the waking state. "You might have eaten to the full and gone to sleep. You dream that you work hard and long in the hot sun all day, are tired and hungry and want to eat a lot."[39] It is true that when "you wake up and find your stomach is full" it has an overall reality which was only temporarily denied by the dream. It does establish the point, however, that each of the three states—waking, dreaming and deep sleep—are capable of contradicting the others. It is thus possible that the experience of reality in

Advaita may do to the waking state what waking does to the dream state. Thus the idea of contradicting knowledge being superior to contradicted knowledge does not close the issue and may even be seen as establishing the possibility that what is now *contradicting* knowledge may through another experience become *contradicted* knowledge. "The main point is, are you prepared, when awake, to affirm the reality of any of your dream experiences? Similarly one who has awakened into ... [reality] cannot affirm the reality of the waking experience. From his viewpoint, the waking state is dream."[40]

Moreover "the psychological correlate of contradiction is an experience of discontinuity."[41] If this is accepted then the following exchange between master and disciple becomes relevant:

> M.: Before we proceed let us make this point clear. Do you not admit that you exist in your sleep?
>
> D.: Yes, I do.
>
> M.: You are the same person that is now awake. Is it not so?
>
> D.: Yes.
>
> M.: So there is continuity in the sleep and the waking states. What is that continuity? It is only the state of Pure Being.[42]

(vii) The claim that the waking state is more real than dream because of its longer duration has already been addressed. In one sense the claim is not even entirely true, for "while dreaming, do we not go through years of experience? You cannot measure dream time by the standard of waking life".[43] Should we do that, however, even then the greater reality of waking over dream is not established. The following exchange between Ramana and a questioner is relevant here:

> D.: But a dream is fleeting and unreal. It is also contradicted by the waking state.
>
> M.: The waking experiences are similar.

D.: One lives fifty years and finds a continuity in the waking experience which is absent in dreams.

M.: You go to sleep and dream a dream in which the experiences of fifty years are condensed within the short duration of the dream, say five minutes. There is also a continuity in the dream. Which is real now? Is the period covering fifty years of your waking state real or the short duration of five minutes of your dream? *The standards of time differ in the two states.* That is all. There is no other difference.[42]

(4) The waking state may be more colourful but that does not make it more real than the others. "The same person sleeps, dreams and wakes up. The waking state is said to be full of beautiful and interesting things. The absence of such experiences makes one say that the sleep state is dull."[45] "The sleep state appears dull because you were not there as an individual and therefore these things were not. But what is the fact? There is the continuity of being in all the three states, but no continuity of the individual and objects."[46]

(5) "The body could not exist without our own existence." Hence it is clear that the body by itself, without existence, cannot be given special status. Besides, we cannot exist in normal life without the body, but we can exist without body-consciousness as in dream and deep sleep. Hence existence is more crucial than *bodily* existence.

(6) Among the states, it was shown earlier, the shorter is remembered in the longer. The waking state is the longest, hence within it dreaming and deep sleep are remembered and not vice versa.

(7) The superior status of perception is by no means clear in the case of the waking state. Curiously, this point emerges both from the traditional Advaitin theory of perception and its scientific criticism. According to Advaita "in all cognition being itself is directly cognised. In every case it is the bare reality . . . that is apprehended, and the activity of the senses is limited to that only: apparent differences in cognitions like 'this is a pot', 'that is a cloth' are illusions . . ." An example may help. In all ornaments of gold it is really gold which is cognized, and inasmuch as the ornaments are seen as different, though they are

all the same as gold, one is a victim of false perception: although the ornaments are made of gold, gold is not an ornament! Thus on the traditional view perception is merely an empirical and not a real phenomenon.

The traditional Advaitin theory of the *process* of perception contains the idea that the mind actually goes out and assumes the shape of the object perceived, thus enabling perception to occur. The interesting point here is that the two main modern critiques of this position serve not merely to challenge the doctrinal Advaitin theory of perception but undermine the very credibility of perception in a way which reinforces the *conclusions* of experiential Advaita even as they challenge its arguments.

Advaita regards perception as direct—that is, simultaneous—but we know "that the sun 'sets' seven minutes before we stop seeing it."[47] In other words, we see a sun which is not there! This does little to confirm our confidence in the waking state. Similarly, according to the Gestalt school, in the process of perception "the structure of the psycho-physical process in the brain is isomorphic with, but remains distinct from, its correlative physical gestalt,"[48] though not so in Advaita. If Advaita is right, empirical perception is suspect from the ultimate point of view; if Gestaltists are right we do not perceive the object, only its representation in some form.

(8) It is not quite true that one does not return to the same suffering in dreams. This happens in the case of recurrent nightmares. Moreover, if the suffering of the waking state is so real, why is it not experienced in deep sleep or dreams? It may be argued that one has pain in deep sleep and dream but is not aware of it. This means that pain characterizes not the body but body-*consciousness* as it comes and goes with it. Pain cannot be dissociated from the *awareness* of pain. This applies both to physical pain and mental distress as the following conversational snippets indicate:

> Q.: What of toothache?
>
> A.: The pain is in the mind, what happens to the toothache during sleep. Do you feel the pain then? No.[49]

*****

Q.: I suffer from worries without end; there is no peace for me, though there is nothing wanting for me to be happy.

A.: Do these worries affect you in sleep?

Q.: No, they do not.

A.: Are you the very same man now, or are you different from him that slept without any worry?

Q.: Yes, I am the same person.

A.: Then surely those worries do not belong to you ...[50]

(9) The perspective is capable of being reversed. One could argue that sleep is the fundamental state, in which waking and dream are disturbances caused by mental agitation. Far from being a mere restorative appendage to waking, deep sleep can afford even more valuable clues to realities than waking. For instance, "in deep sleep man is devoid of possessions, including his own body. Instead of being unhappy he is quite happy. Everyone desires to sleep soundly. The conclusion is that happiness is inherent in man and is not due to external causes."[51]

(10) It is true that in the waking state the maximum exercise of volition is possible. But it is also possible in dreaming where one might face a decision-making situation. Moreover, it is definitely possible in the case of lucid dreams or dreams in which one is aware that one is dreaming. And if the waking state is considered analogous to dreaming this turns the tables—for waking could be nothing more than lucid dreaming, only we may not know it to be such. The devastating effects of sleep-deprivation on the waking state are also well-documented. So in a sense the waking state as characterized by volition cannot be divorced from deep sleep.

(11) It is our mind which says that there was unconsciousness in sleep, implying that the kind of consciousness which is characteristic of the mind—namely, one involving the division of subject and object—was not present therein. In terms of the mind there was no consciousness as the mind knows it, just as one who is colour-blind sees no colour even though it is there but falls outside the range of shades the person can see. "It is only

you who say dreamless sleep is empty of all consciousness after waking from sleep; you do not say so while actually asleep. That is the you which now says that sleep is unconsciousness of your mind. But it was not present in your sleep, and it is natural for the mind to be ignorant of the consciousness that is in sleep. Not having experienced sleep, it is unable to remember what it was like, and makes mistakes about it. The state of deep sleep is beyond the mind."[52]

The preceding analysis may have been rather detailed. Some points of a more general nature in the Advaitin critique of our normal experience may be emphasized: (1) that waking and dreaming are not as opposed to each other analytically as they seem to be perceptually and (2) that the state of sleep is philosophically of far greater importance than may be physically apparent. These points will now be elaborated.

Many thinkers—both Eastern and Western—have felt that drawing a firm distinction between waking and dreaming presents difficulties. Among Western thinkers Descartes and Pascal may be specially mentioned. Descartes wrote:

> When I consider the matter carefully, I do not find a single characteristic by means of which I can certainly determine whether I am awake or whether I am dreaming. The visions of a dream and the experiences of my waking state are so much alike that I am completely puzzled and I do not really know if I am not dreaming at this moment.[53]

And Pascal said:

> If a dream comes to us every night we should be as much occupied with it as by the thing we see every day, and if an artisan were certain that he would dream every night for twelve hours that he was a king, then he would be just as happy as a king who dreams every night for twelve hours that he is an artisan.[54]

In the East, the Indian king Janaka and the Chinese philosopher Chuan-Tzu were baffled, it seems, by similar experiences. There was once a famous Indian king called Janaka. "King Janaka had a dream that he was a beggar. On his waking up he asked his guru . . . 'Am I a king dreaming of being a beggar or a beggar dreaming of being a king?' "[55]

Chuan-Tzu (*c.* 369-286 B.C.), second in importance only to Lao-Tzu as a representative of Taoism, raises for "epistemology . . . the ultimately unanswerable question":[56]

> Once upon a time, Chuan Chou [i.e. Chuang Tzu] dreamed that he was a butterfly, a butterfly fluttering about, enjoying itself. It did not know that it was Chuang Chou. Suddenly he awoke with a start and he was Chuang Chou again. But he did not know whether he was Chuang Chou who had dreamed that he was a butterfly, or whether he was a butterfly dreaming that he was Chuang Chou. Between Chuang Chou and the butterfly there must be some distinction. This is what is called the transformation of things.[57]

In a less celebrated and more elaborate passage Chuan-Tzu further considers the plausibility of the dream-like nature of life. "Those who dream of a merry drinking party may the next morning wail and weep. Those who dream of wailing and weeping may in the morning go off gaily to hunt. While they dream they do not know that they are dreaming. In their dream, they may even try to interpret their dream. Only when they have awakened do they begin to know that they have dreamed. By and by comes the great awakening, and then we shall know that it has all been a great dream. Yet all the while the fools think that they are awake; this they are sure of. With minute nicety, they discriminate between princes and grooms. How stupid! Confucius and you are both in a dream. And when I say that you are in a dream, this is also a dream. This way of talking may be called paradoxical. If after ten thousand generations we could once meet a great sage who knew how to explain the paradox, it would be as though we met him after only one morning or one evening."[58]

A similar tendency to treat the waking state as analogous to dreaming also appears in Buddhist thought, as the following passage indicates:

> The senses are as though illusions and their objects as dreams. For instance a sleeping man might dream that he had made love to a beautiful country girl, and he might remember her when he awoke. What do you think— ... does the beautiful girl he dreamed of really exist?"

> "No, Lord."
>
> "And would the man be wise to remember the girl of his dreams, or to believe that he had really made love to her?"
>
> "No, Lord, because she doesn't really exist at all, so how could he have made love to her—though of course he might think he did under the influence of weakness or fatigue."
>
> "In just the same way a foolish and ignorant man of the world sees pleasant forms and believes in their existence. Hence he is pleased, and so he feels passion and acts accordingly...[59]

Mystics even more than philosophers are inclined to disregard the distinction, at some level, between waking and dreaming, as in the following story narrated by Ramakrsna (1836-1886).[60] "A son was born to a king. He was the only child and was therefore 'the apple of the eye' of both the king and the queen. The prince became a favourite with all and as he grew older he was taught all the arts and the sciences. One day, all of a sudden, the prince fell ill. The malady went on getting worse and even the best physician of the kingdom found that all treatments were of no avail. Both the king and the queen never left his side day and night and the most competent physician and nurses continuously attended on him. The king was exhausted by his constant vigil and one night he could not resist falling asleep. He was awakened by the sound of crying and weeping and learnt that the prince had passed away while he was asleep. The king sat as if he was stupefied, without speaking a single word. The queen asked him how it was that on the passing away of the only child whom he loved so much there was not a single drop of tear in his eyes. The king said, 'Oh queen, when I fell asleep I dreamt that I had become the monarch of a large kingdom, much larger than mine, and the father of seven worthy and ideal princes, each of whom was well trained in the art of administration. I handed over the charge of my kingdom to them and thereafter I was spending my days in peace and happiness with you. And now this tragedy has taken place and I am unable to make up my mind whether I should lament for the child that has left us today or whether I should mourn the loss of the seven sons and a vast kingdom. I see no difference in the two bereavements and to me the world has become nothing but a dream.'"[61]

By contrast Ramana Maharshi (d. 1950) asserts even more directly the elusiveness of the distinction. "All that we see is a dream, whether we see it in the dream state or waking state. On account of some arbitrary standards about the duration of the experience and so on, we call one experience a dream and another waking experience. With reference to reality both the experiences are unreal. A man might have such an experience as getting *anugraha* (grace) in his dream and the effects and influence of it on his entire subsequent life may be so profound and so abiding that one cannot call it unreal, while calling real some trifling incident in the waking life that just flits by, is casual and of no moment and is soon forgotten. Once I had an experience, a vision or a dream, whatever you may call it. I and some others including Chadwick had a walk on the hill. Returning we were walking along a huge street with great buildings on either side. Showing the street and the buildings, I asked Chadwick and others whether anybody could say that what we were seeing was dream and they all replied, 'Which fool will say so?' and we walked along and entered the hall and the vision or dream ceased, or [we] woke up. What are we to call this?"[62]

While on the one hand the distinction between waking and dreaming is blurred, on the other the significance of deep sleep is emphasized and clarified. The crucial point to note here is that in deep sleep *both the awareness of our individuality and of the world is lost, and yet our sense of identity survives this loss of individuality.* This is considered by Advaitins as truly phenomenal: that our identity can be independent of our personality or individuality. In the following extended conversation three key ideas developed in the light of the Advaitin analysis of ordinary experience—(1) that the world may be in us rather than we being in the world; (2) that the world may be a dream-world rather than us dreaming within a world; and (3) that deep sleep may provide a clue to our true identity—are all brought together:

M.: Are you in the world? Or is the world in you?

D.: I do not understand. The world is certainly around me.

M.: You speak of the world and happenings in it. They are mere ideas in you. The ideas are in the mind. The mind is within you. And so the world is within you.

D.: I do not follow you. Even if I do not think of the world, the world is still there.

M.: Do you mean to say that the world is apart from the mind and it can exist in the absence of the mind?

D.: Yes.

M.: Does the world exist in your deep sleep?

D.: It does.

M.: Do you see it in your sleep?

D.: No, I don't. But others, who are awake, see it.

M.: Are you so aware in your sleep? Or do you become aware of the other's knowledge now?

D.: In my waking state.

M.: So you speak of waking knowledge and not of sleep-experiences. The existence of the world in your waking and dream states is admitted because they are the products of the mind. The mind is withdrawn in sleep and the world is in the condition of a seed. It becomes manifest over again when you wake up. The ego springs forth, identifies itself with the body and sees the world. So the world is a mental creation.

D.: How can it be?

M.: Do you not create a world in your dream? The waking state also is a long drawn out dream. There must be a seer behind the waking and dream experiences. Who is that seer? Is it the body?

D.: It cannot be.

M.: Is it the mind?

D.: It must be so.

M.: But you remain in the absence of the mind.

D.: How?

M.: In deep sleep.

D.: I do not know if I am then.

M.: If you were not how do you recollect yesterday's experiences? Is it possible that there was a break in the continuity of the 'I' during sleep?

D.: It may be.

M.: If so, a Johnson may wake up as a Benson. How will the identity of the individual be established?

D.: I don't know.

M.: If this argument is not clear, follow a different line. You admit "I slept well", "I feel refreshed after a sound sleep". So sleep was your experience. The experiencer now identifies himself with the 'I' in the speaker. So this 'I' must have been in sleep also.

D.: Yes.

M.: So 'I' was in sleep; if the world was then there, did it say that it existed?

D.: No. But the world tells me its existence now. Even if I deny its existence, I may knock myself against a stone and hurt my foot. The injury proves the existence of the stone and so of the world.

M.: Quite so. The stone hurts the foot. Does the foot say that there is the stone?

D.: No.—'I'.

M.: Who is this 'I'? It cannot be the body nor the mind as we have seen before. This 'I' is the one who experiences the waking, dream and sleep states. The three states

> are changes which do not affect the individual. The experiences are like pictures passing on a screen in the cinema. The appearance and disappearance of the pictures do not affect the screen. So also, the three states alternate with one another leaving the Self unaffected. The waking and the dream states are creations of the mind. So the Self covers all. To know that the Self remains happy in its perfection is Self-Realisation. Its use lies in the realisation of Perfection and thus of Happiness.[63]

These various considerations amount to this: that whereas in terms of ordinary living and experience the waking state does occupy a "vantage-point ... genuine philosophical inquiry should not be restricted to the implications of waking state alone, for waking is only a segment of experience. And, inquiry in order to be fruitful must take into account the total experience. It is thus that the inquiry into the three states becomes supremely important..."[64]

CHAPTER III

CONCLUSIONS BASED ON THE CRITIQUE OF NORMAL EXPERIENCE

I

Advaita is concerned with examining ordinary experience from the standpoint of reality. What then is reality? According to Advaita "reality must always be real."[65] Or, in other words, *reality must always be.*

Now can it be said of any of the states experienced by human beings—waking, dreaming or deep sleep—that they always are? Quite manifestly this is not the case. "One experiences a dream and knows it to be unreal on waking. Waking experience is unreal in other states. So each state contradicts the others."[66] None of these three states, therefore, represents reality by itself.

Is there, however, something which is always present in these three states? Advaita suggests that *you* are present in all the three states:

> In saying 'I had a dream; I was in deep sleep; I am awake', you must admit that you were there in all the three states. That makes it clear that you were there all the time. If you remain as you are now, you are in the wakeful state; this becomes hidden in the dream state; and the dream state disappears when you are in deep sleep. You were there then, you are there now, and you are there at all times. The three states come and go, but you are always there.[67]

At this point it becomes necessary to distinguish between the 'I' and the 'I-thought'. When we say 'I had a dream' etc., the 'I' here stands for the 'I-thought' or the ego.

The fact that although the three states are discontinuous and contradict each other, and are yet experienced with a sense of connectedness suggests that there must be some subject which is witnessing these states; otherwise the sense of identity through them could not persist. It is also obvious that this subject must be *different* from these three states, *although* witnessing them. Its "existence is deduced from the principle that what knows must be other than what is known."[68] "Nothing, it is said, can be the subject as well as the object of one and the same action. The eye can see other things, but not itself. The finger's end can touch other objects, but not itself."[69]

Two points here need to be clearly recognized: (1) that the subject is *always* present within these three states of ordinary experience otherwise the experience cannot occur (as all experience involves an experiencing subject) yet (2) it is *never* experienced as the *pure* subject so often referred to as the *self* as it is always implicated in experience. It is in this sense that:

> Realisation is ever present, not absent at one time and present at another. For example the Sun does not see darkness. But others speak of darkness fleeing at his approach. Similarly ignorance is a phantom; when its unreal nature is found, it is said to be removed. Again the sun is there and you are surrounded by sunlight, but to know this you must turn your eyes in his direction and look at him. So also the Self is found by practice alone, although it is here and now.

II

This creates the peculiar situation that the subject is both known and unknown. It is known as *always* implicated in experience but, on that very account, *never* known as the pure subject. According to Advaita the pure subject is our true self whose knowledge is liberative, while all the while we function with the objectified self—that is, with a self which is the subject in a subject-object relationship in the course of ordinary living. If the subject could be realised in its *purity* then all misery would cease: this is called self-knowledge "and self-knowledge is unique in that the knowing self is itself the known self. It can never become a known or unknown object."[71] It can never become a *known* object because as soon as it is known in the ordinary sense it is objectified and loses its status as the pure subject; it can never remain unknown, however, as all knowledge implies the existence of a subject. Advaita claims that "there is only one consciousness subsisting in the states of waking, dream and sleep. In sleep, there is no 'I'; thought arises on waking and then the world appears. Where was this 'I' in sleep? Was it there or was it not? *It must have been there also, but not in the way that you feel now*. The sleeping 'I' is the real 'I' that subsists all through. That is consciousness. If that is known, you will see that it is beyond thoughts."[72]

But how does one turn one's face towards the sun?

The first point to keep in mind is the fact that, to begin with, one establishes its existence. If one sees light all around, and one not only sees light all around but also sees *in* the light all around, then one, on the basis of this experience, logically posits a source of this light—on the basis of a rational analysis of the experience of seeing. It is important to note that the positing of the source *precedes* the search for the source, a search which leads to the actual realization of the source. The source is not seen to begin with, it is seen only subsequently.

One must recognize not only the *priority* of the postulation but also the sense of *discovery* which accompanies the direct visual realization of the source; in this case, the sun. It is as if an astronomer were to survey the movement of the heavenly bodies and chart their gravitational pulls. After poring over the various equations, he concludes that all the astronomical facts can only be fully accounted for by positing an additional heavenly body which has not yet been identified. On the basis of this rational conviction he proceeds to surmise where in the sky this body was likely to be located on the basis of his calculations. And then he turns a telescope in that direction and spots it!

Advaita seems to function in a similar manner. Only its universe of discourse is the ordinary experience of human life. It analyses human experience as divisible into three states; waking, dreaming and deep sleep. *All* that we experience as a human being is experienced within one of these three states. But *these three states represent different kinds of experience according to its analysis, not just different experiences within one state—namely waking—as we may be uncritically inclined to believe*. But then the question arises: If the experiences are different then how do they all seem to pertain to the same entity—especially when the three states in some ways differ so radically? In waking we experience a physical body and physical objects; in dreaming we sometimes find a dream-body and experience objects which on waking turn out to have been only mental; and in deep sleep there is no empirical experience: we are aware neither of ourselves or of the world. Yet we say *I* am awake, *I* dreamt and *I* slept. What is the nature of this subject which keeps experiencing but which we never directly experience? We only experience it as an experiencer, never as experienced.

Advaita suggests that it is possible to know it, but never as the experienced. For in order for anything to be experienced, it must have an experien*cer*, which is what the subject is by definition! This paradoxical situation is referred to in Advaita as the property of the self-luminosity of the self, something like the power of the sight of the eyes, which see but cannot see themselves, and yet whose existence cannot be denied, otherwise one couldn't see at all. It should now be clear why this self-luminosity of the self is defined in Advaita as "the capacity of being called immediately known in empirical usage while not being an object of cognition."[73]

Advaita tells us: "You have been so accustomed to objectivity that you have lost the knowledge of yourself, simply because the self cannot be objectified."[74] The problem is that we *always* experience the 'I' as a subject connected with objects in the waking and dreaming states, or do not *experience it at all* as in deep sleep when *both* subjects and objects disappear. What one needs to do is to experience the 'I' as pure subject, not as 'subjectified' in relation to an object.

This then is the second major movement of thought which characterizes experiential Advaita. The first major movement of thought called for a re-examination of the categories of ordinary experience: waking, dreaming and deep sleep. This movement of thought questioned these distinctions as we ordinarily draw them, regarding dreaming and deep sleep as appendages to the waking state. This was done by questioning the conventional distinction on the one hand between waking and dreaming as opposite types of experience and by indicating the philosophical significance of sleep on the other.[75] Now this second movement of thought highlights the discontinuity between these states, especially waking-dreaming and deep sleep, but also indicates the rational necessity of positing a common subject underlying this discontinuity, in the absence of which the three separate and disparate states could not possibly constitute the experience of a single person.

III

This second movement of thought necessitates a third: a re-examination of the analysis of the three states in order to indicate both *what* is the nature of this pure subject which is being sought and *how* it might be discovered. This dual thrust of the fresh analysis of the three states is the clear implication, for instance, of some of the remarks by Ramana. On the one hand he admits that in a sense deep sleep is closer to the state of the pure subject as "the sleep state is free from thoughts and their impression on the individual."[76] Yet, at the same time, he warns that "one should not therefore desire to be always in sleep" because the "incentive to realise" the self can "arise only in the waking state and efforts can only be made when one is awake."[77]

This distinction between *what* is to be realized and *how* it is to be realized is crucial to an understanding of the way these three states of waking, dreaming and deep sleep are approached in experiential Advaita. In effect these three states are set up in a pattern of opposing hierarchies (one might even say structure and anti-structure) by Ramana and earlier thinkers of Advaita; one may designate the former as a theoretical and the latter as a practical approach. "The theoretical approach shows us where we want to go, i.e., to the interiorization and unification of consciousness, while the practical approach indicates the means to achieve that end, i.e., through Advaitic knowledge of yogic will."[78]

The theoretical approach may be elaborated first. It could be argued that as one moves from the waking state progressively to dreaming and deep sleep in terms of ordinary experience, consciousness becomes increasingly subjectified in the empirical subject. In the waking state objects are external to the subject, who is distinct from them. In dreams, the objects become a product of the person's interior consciousness. They are within the subject. In deep sleep, the distinction between the subject and the object dissolves—even the internal division within a dream between the experiencing subject and the experienced objects vanishes. All that is left is the sleeping person. But as on waking up the person remembers having slept, there must have been some conscious subject which witnessed the unconsciousness of sleep. This pure subject has to be realized. Its realization is said to put an end to all unhappiness. Such is the Advaitin claim, that except for one who experientially comes to "know" this pure subject, which "is known solely by means of itself"[79] on account of its self-luminosity, "every man, from king to peasant has a certain amount of sorrow. Even in cases where it seems absent it is only a time factor that makes you think so—sooner or later it comes."[80] So says Ramana.

This analysis is suggestive in several ways. First, it suggests that a radical discontinuity is involved in realizing the pure subject, on account of its purity: its total absence of any relationship with any object either in the sense of identification with object as in deep sleep, interiorized relationship as in dreams or an external relation as in the waking state. Thus the knowledge of the pure subject is *categorically* different from the knowledge or absence of it which arises in a subject-object context, even though this latter type of knowledge is itself *qualitatively* different in waking, dreaming and deep sleep. Second, as the realization of pure subjectivity entails the total elimination of any form of object-contextuality, the realization of the pure subject is a purely negative enterprise in the sense that all objects have to be eliminated at all levels—including the possibility of a subject in *relation* to no objects. The subject must *be* just that. "When non-self disappears, the self alone remains. To make room it is enough that cramping is removed. Space is not brought in afresh. Nay more, space is there even in cramping."[81] This passage serves to explain the comment that while in ordinary experience the "true self cannot be known" "it does not therefore remain unrealized, for it is self-revealing. In fact it can never be wholly suppressed."[82] It is in this sense perhaps that one must understand Ramana's remark: "The feeling that I have not realised is the obstruction to realisation. In fact, it is already realised ...."[83]

The practical approach towards the realization of the self and its relation to the three states of waking, dreaming and deep sleep may now be examined. Any effort at realization involves volition, so from a *practical* point of view the hierarchy is reversed: no volition is possible in deep sleep, perhaps more in dreaming but most in the waking state!

IV

What, it might be asked, is the exact nature of the problem towards solving which efforts must be directed in the waking state?

The problem is best illustrated with the help of an example. Let us take the case of a young lady who is in love with her beau and goes out to buy a nice dress to please him. She brings the dress home and places it on the table. She then reclines on the chair and begins to speculate on the romantic possibilities this addition to her wardrobe could set in motion.

She imagines how she will wear the dress in the evening and go out for a candlelit dinner with her friend. She will iron the dress with particular care and wear a perfume with it. She imagines the possibility of spilling wine on it and spoiling the dress (God forbid), and how she will preserve it and after years of marriage still keep it though it may be worn out, and how she will show it to her daughter as the dress she wore on the evening her husband proposed to her. While she is thus thinking, the phone rings and she talks to her friend about this fabulous dress she bought in the morning, describing in great detail the way it came to be purchased.

Throughout this series of events the actual dress has simply been lying on the table. So all her experiences do not really pertain to the dress but to the *dress-thought*. When she thinks of wearing the dress it is really the *dress-thought* she is concerned with—the dress as such is merely lying on the table. The web of romantic associations she has woven are also woven not around the dress itself, which just lies as an item on the table, but around the *dress-thought*, in her mind. When she talks with her friend on the phone she really talks of the *dress-thought*, not the dress itself which lies on the table and is indifferent to the vicissitudes of fortune the *dress-thought* is undergoing. The moment the lady stops thinking or talking of the *dress-thought*—which is what is really involved in the thinking or talking about it rather than the dress itself—the *dress-thought* may be said to go back into the dress, as it were.

This example serves to illustrate several aspects of the problem at hand. It is the Advaitin contention that what we are concerned with in the process of ordinary living is not the real 'I' but the 'I-thought', just as what the lady was concerned with in exploring her romantic situation was the dress-*thought* and not the dress, even though she may find it difficult to draw this distinction at all. Although the dress as dress-thought was the object of so much activity, the dress as such just lay passively on the table. It is the Advaitin contention that just as it was not the dress but the dress-*thought* which ran the young lady's life for a while, it is not the pure subject—the pure 'I'—but the 'I-thought' which runs our lives, divorced from the real 'I' but deriving its existence from it, just as the dress-thought is divorced from the dress and yet derives its existence from it! This 'I-thought' is also called the ego and it is said that "those alone who have found out the real nature of the ego have seen reality. They will have no more doubts or anxiety."[84] Even this point can be clarified analogically: just as once one has discovered the nature of the dress-thought—which one constantly confused with the dress itself—one would also discover the real nature of the dress as such, unclouded by the dress-thought.

In Advaita it is said that realization of one's true nature entails realizing how the 'I-thought' *rises* from the real 'I'. "To say 'I am this' or 'I am that' there must be the 'I'. This 'I' is only the ego or the 'I-thought'. After the rising up of this 'I-thought' all other thoughts arise. The 'I-thought' is therefore the root-thought . . . find out its source. Then all these [other thoughts] will vanish and the pure self will remain over."[85] Similarly one is told that the ego proceeds from the self as a spark from fire. "The spark is called the ego. In the case of the ignorant man it identifies itself with an object simultaneously with its rise. It cannot remain independent of such association with objects ... If its objectifying tendency is killed it remains pure and also merges into the source."[86] This point can also be made in relation to the analogy of the dress-thought and the dress. When we perceive the dress *qua* dress without dress-thoughts one can describe the process as either *tracing* dress-thoughts back to their source, the dress, or making dress-thoughts *merge* into the dress.

Just as one needed to distinguish between the dress and the dress-thought, one needs to distinguish between the 'I' and the 'I-thought'. "You must distinguish between the 'I', pure in itself, and the 'I'-thought."[87] "If you stay as the 'I', your being alone, without thought, the 'I'-thought will disappear and the delusion will vanish forever."[88]

This raises the interesting question: are there two 'I's? The parallel question in terms of the analogy would be—are there two dresses? There is only one dress. Similarly, there is only one 'I'. But just as the dress gives rise to the dress-thought, the 'I-thought' emerges from the 'I'. Or, one can even say that once the dress-thought has arisen, several dress-thoughts in various phases arise based on the original dress-thought. This helps explain the following: "the 'I' of the dream has vanished. Another 'I' speaks of the dream. This 'I' was not in the dream. Both the 'I's are unreal. There is the substratum of the mind which continues all along, giving rise to so many scenes. With every thought arises 'I', and with its disappearance that 'I' disappears too. So the 'I's are born, and die every moment,"[89] like dress-thoughts emerging from moment to moment. Once one knows that the dress is lying safely on the table the vicissitudes of the dress-thoughts cease to be a cause for concern.

There are other ways as well in which the analogy of the dress and dress-thought is illuminating. For instance, it is said in Advaita: "that which makes the enquiry is the ego. The 'I' about which the enquiry is made is also the ego. As a result of the enquiry the ego ceases to exist."[90] Parallel: starting as we do from the realm of dress-thought, it is the dress-thought which enquires *into* itself. Then it realizes it is just the dress-thought and disappears, yielding place to the actual dress lying on the table. Again, in Advaita one is encouraged to enquire who undergoes the vicissitudes of life and to discover that only the ego is affected by them, not the self, and that "the ego is non-existent."[91] Parallel: the dress-thought undergoes all the vicissitudes, the dress itself is not bound by them and the dress-thought is non-existent in the sense that what really exists is only the dress. Again it is said: "reality is simply the loss of ego." Parallel: the recognition of the reality of the dress is simply the loss of dress-thoughts. Thus the analogy is helpful in many ways. Let me close by pointing out two more instances in which it is helpful in a much more dynamic sense—in shedding light on the actual pursuit of the spiritual goal.

It is sometimes said that the realization could be sudden or gradual, that is, taking time to steady itself. At times Ramana said that "there are no degrees of liberation,"[92] and at other times that "realization takes time to steady itself."[93] This could also be understood in terms of our analogy. Let us imagine that the young lady in the parable is suddenly told that her beau has run off with someone else! If the lady is shocked to her senses by this revelation the dress would immediately become a piece of cloth for her—the dress-thoughts would disappear. If, however, she still retained affection for the heel who left her, dress-thoughts might still occasionally arise from the dress and may only gradually subside till the dress becomes just a piece of cloth (that is, till she finds another beau).

It is also sometimes said that realization is not possible so long as till one is "aware *of* an 'I' "; it is only possible upon "*being* the 'I' ". So long as one has thoughts *of* the dress, one is in a sense in a state of alienation from the dress and still in the realm of dress-thoughts. But when the dress becomes the dress—that is, when all dress-thoughts disappear, then alone it is in its natural and primal state.

The process of realization may be said to consist of three stages. In the first stage one is aware of only the 'I-thought' to begin with. One is so carried away by this identification with the 'I-thought' that one does not know there is an underlying real 'I' which is quite *different* from the 'I-thought', although the source of it. In other words, the pure subject, though ever present, is never known because of one's identification of existence with the three states of waking, dreaming and deep sleep. As it is precisely this world represented by the three states which conceals the pure witness, one must, in the second stage, lose sight of the world to experience the pure subject. As Ramana explains in this catechetical series:

> *When will the realization of the self be gained?* When the world which is what-is-seen has been removed, there will be realization of the self which is the seer.
> *Will there not be the realization of the self even while the world is there (taken as real)?* There will not be.[94]

In the third stage, once the pure subject is realized, the world is again seen but now as part of the self and not apart from it as was the case in the beginning. In terms of our analogy one begins with the bride with her mind full of dress-thoughts. In stage two she experiences the actual dress to be worn. She cannot see it unless the dress-thoughts depart from the mind so that she can see and experience the actual dress. While actually experiencing it even the thought "this is the dress" is a distraction from it. Finally, emerging from the absorption in the dress she can again lose herself in dress-thoughts going down the aisle—but she is aware of the relationship of these dress-thoughts to the real dress, which was not the case the first time.

V

How, then, does one move from the 'I-thought' or the ego in which we now live and move and have our being, to the realization of the pure 'I' or the pure subject? The method is compactly and concisely presented by Ramana:

> Arranging thoughts in the order of value, the 'I-thought is the all-important thought. Personality-idea or thought is also the root or the stem of all other thoughts, since each idea or thought arises only as someone's thought and is not known to exist independently of the ego. The ego therefore exhibits thought-activity. The second and the third persons [he, you, that, etc.] do not appear except to the first person [I]. Therefore they arise only after the first person appears, so all the three persons seem to rise and sink together. Trace, then, the ultimate cause of 'I' or personality.
>
> From where does this 'I' arise? Seek for it within; it then vanishes. This is the pursuit of wisdom. When the mind unceasingly investigates its own nature, it transpires that there is no such thing as mind. This is the direct path for all. The mind is merely thoughts. Of all thoughts the thought 'I' is the root. Therefore the mind is only the thought 'I'.
>
> The birth of the 'I'-thought is one's own birth, its death is the person's death. After the 'I'-thought has arisen, the wrong identity with the body arises. Get rid of the 'I'-thought. So long as 'I' is alive there is grief. When 'I' ceases to exist there is no grief.[95]

This, however, is to be followed up with another step:

> You must distinguish between the 'I', pure in itself, and the 'I'-thought. The latter, being merely a thought, sees subject and object, sleeps, wakes up, eats and thinks . . . . But the pure 'I' is the pure being, eternal existence, free from ignorance and thought-illusion. If you stay as the 'I', your being alone, without thought, the 'I'-thought will disappear and the delusion will vanish for ever.[96]

Once this delusion has vanished, life is

> like a cinema. The screen is always there but several types of pictures appear on the screen and then disappear. Nothing sticks to the screen, it remains a screen. Similarly, you remain your own Self in all the three states. If you know that, the three states will not trouble you, just as the pictures which appear on the screen do not stick to it. On the screen, you sometimes see a huge ocean with endless waves; that disappears. Another time, you see fire spreading all around; that too disappears. The screen is there on both occasions. Did the screen get wet with the water or did it get burned by the fire? Nothing affected the screen. In the same way, the things that happen during the wakeful, dream and sleep states do not affect you at all; you remain your own Self.[97]

CHAPTER IV

ADVAITIN EXPERIENCE AND ITS RELATIONSHIP TO NORMAL EXPERIENCE

I

The Advaitin claim is based on experience, but it is based on the experience of a chosen few. This by itself need not induce scepticism; after all, the claims of nuclear physics are based on the experiments of a chosen few. What is more, its conclusions are as much at odds with ordinary experience as the concept of a spherical earth with our everyday experience of it as flat when we walk on it. Nuclear physicists, for instance, would have us believe that the solid, stable table I am writing on at the moment is full of empty subatomic spaces and in a state of atomic flux. There is at least something to be said for this: "that our sole warrant for speaking about reality is experience and that, when experience vouches for such a character, it must be admitted to be so. The so-called contradictions may themselves be the ultimate truth about reality. Thought must follow the nature of reality in grasping it, and should not attempt to determine it."[98]

II

In what ways, then, does the Advaitin experience of reality contrast with the ordinary experience of it?

In many ways the realized being continues to be an ordinary being. He or she will feel a slap when struck; "a man under chloroform or drink does not feel a slap" and that does not make him a realized person. Realization "is not inconsistent with the feeling of a slap".[99] A realized person also has dreams.[100] The realized person also experiences the world. He or she can "move about and act and speak,"[101] like ordinary human beings do.

The realized person, however, in a sense experiences less than the ordinary person; in another sense experiences more than the ordinary person; and in yet another sense experiences the world differently from an ordinary person.

III

The realized person experiences pain and pleasure but does not experience it in the same way as an ordinary person. "The sensation is common both to the realized man and the unrealized. The difference is that the unrealized man identifies himself with the body that feels it." The realized one has the attitude: "If there is pain let it be; it is also part of the self and the self is perfect."[102] In a sense it might be said that the realized person feels physical pain but not mental pain. It could also be said that the difference between a realized person and an ordinary person does not lie so much in what the realized one experiences and the ordinary one does not but rather in what the ordinary person experiences and the realized one does not. The realized person and the ordinary person both experience sugar as sweet and wormwood as bitter, both see and smell and walk and talk.[103] But the ordinary person also experiences anxiety, fear, suffering, hope, disappointment etc. These the realized person does not experience.[104]

What about his attitude to the pain of others? Once Ramana was asked, "When we suffer grief and complain and appeal to you by letter or mentally by prayer, are you not moved to feel what a pity it is that your child suffers like this?" He replied: "If one felt like that one would not be a realized person!"[105] This may sound callous but only if it is misunderstood. One needs to be reminded here of what Ramana repeatedly said: "that if one realises the self one will know that all suffering, not just one's own, is non-existent."[106] When asked, "We see pain in the world. A man is hungry. It is a physical reality and as such very real to him. Are we to call it a dream and remain unmoved by his pain?", Ramana explained that from the point of view of realization of reality:

> the pain you speak of is certainly a dream, as is the world of which the pain is an infinitesimal part. In the dream also you yourself feel hunger. You see others suffering hunger. You feed yourself and, moved by pity, feed the others that you find suffering from hunger. So long as the dream lasts, all those hunger pains are quite as real as you now think the pain you see in the world to be. It is only when you wake up that you discover that the pain in the dream was unreal. You might have eaten to the full and gone to sleep. You dream that you work hard and long in the hot sun all day, are tired and hungry and want to eat a lot. Then you get up and find your stomach is full and you have not stirred out of your bed. But all this is not to say that while you are in the dream you can act as if the pain you feel there is not real. The hunger in the dream has to be assuaged by the food in the dream. The fellow beings you found so hungry in the dream had to be provided with food in that dream. You can never mix up the two states, the dream and the waking state.[107]

Ramana goes on to say in the passage that one must "do social service to relieve suffering whenever you see it"[108] *until* realization is attained but even here there is need for caution. Ramana is known to have cried when he heard of the misfortunes of others.[109] In fact he states that the realized ones "do things for the sake of others with detachment, without themselves being affected by them."[110]

In a word, the realized one *experiences* what an ordinary person does but does not *suffer* as he does, having realized his identity as the pure subject. Whereas the ordinary person sees himself *only* within the dream, the realized one can say: "I am both inside and outside the dream. Just as a man having headache knows the ache and also knows that he is not the ache, so do I know the dream, myself dreaming and myself not dreaming—all at the same time. I am what I am before, during and after the dream. But what I see in dream, I am not."[111]

IV

It is apparent from the above that the realized one experiences *less* than the ordinary person (in terms of mental anguish, for instance) because he has experienced *more* (of the pure subject) than the ordinary person.

He experiences more than the ordinary person in that while he experiences the three states like the ordinary person he also realizes that they are unreal. But the ordinary person is "unable to comprehend this, because for him the standard of reality is the waking state,"[112] while for the realized "the standard of reality is reality itself. This reality ... subsists equally during what you call waking, dreaming and sleep."[113]

> When the Realized Man sees the world he sees the Self that is the substratum of all that is seen. Whether the unrealized man sees the world or not, he is ignorant of his true being, the Self. Take the example of a film on a cinema screen. What is there in front of you before the film begins? Only the screen. On that screen you see the entire show, and to all appearances the pictures are real. But go and try to take hold of them and what do you take hold of? The screen on which the pictures appear so real. After the play, when the

> pictures disappear, what remains? The screen again. So it is with the Self. That alone exists; the pictures come and go. If you hold on to the Self, you will not be deceived by the appearance of the pictures. Nor does it matter at all whether the pictures appear or disappear.[114]

Certain other metaphors may also be employed to elaborate the point. The world is "seen by both" the realized and the ordinary person but "their view-points differ"[115] inasmuch as the realized person has a more comprehensive picture subsequent to the realization of the pure subject. The ordinary person only sees the reflection in the mirror but the realized person sees the reflection as well as the mirror."For instance you see a reflection in the mirror and the mirror. You know the mirror to be the reality and the picture in it a mere reflection. Is it necessary that to see the mirror we should cease to see the reflection in it?"[116] Similarly, the realized one continues to experience the world in his realized state. Thus the realized person appreciates "the distinctions" of sound, taste, form, smell etc. "But he *always* perceives and experiences the one reality in all of them. That is why he has no preferences. Whether he moves about, talks, or acts, it is all one reality in which he acts or moves or talks."[117]

In fact three stages may be distinguished in the interest of clarity. To begin with an ordinary person sees only the world. Then he withdraws his consciousness from the world, which is voided, so to say, so that he may realize the pure subject. Subsequently he sees the world again but now with pure consciousness as the substratum.

V

The experience of the realized person is both less and more than that of the ordinary person; it is also bound to be different. This difference turns on a crucial aspect which tends to take one beyond the confines of Western psychology. In Western psychology consciousness is always considered to be intentional; that is to say, consciousness is always consciousness of something. Ramana claims that the experience of the pure subject or the self involves "conciousness without content."[118] He goes on to say: "The Western psychologists who deny this and say consciousness must have an object are quite correct, so far as the individual and mental consciousness is concerned"[119] but "they are incorrect"[120] when they apply this belief to the pure subject which is realized *after* shedding individuality. Thus while waking, dreaming and deep sleep are states of consciousness, the pure subject or self which represents pure consciousness and its realization is radically distinct from these states. Even though they differ from each other, they nevertheless represent modifications of consciousness. When asked: "Is it possible to be conscious without thought?", Ramana replied: "Yes."[121]

The idea is so strange to us who are accustomed to functioning only in states of ordinary experience that an example may be required to illustrate its possibility. When Nisargadatta talked about pure consciousness or contentless consciousness or said that reality cannot be found in states *of* consciousness, he was asked: "Sir, of what use to me is your telling me .. [all this]? Where else am I to look for it? How do you apprehend it?". He replied:

> It is quite simple. If I ask you what is the taste of your mouth, all you can do is to say: it is neither sweet nor bitter, nor sour nor astringent; it is what remains when all these tastes are not. Similarly, when all distinctions and reactions are no more, what remains is reality, simple and solid.[122]

Ramana addressed the fear of many about pure consciousness when he remarked:

> People are afraid that when the ego or the mind is killed, the result may be a mere blank and not happiness. What really happens is that the thinker, the object of thought and thinking all merge in the one Source which is Consciousness and Bliss itself, and thus that state is neither inert nor blank. I don't understand why people should be afraid of a state in which all thoughts cease to exist and the mind is killed. They daily experience it in sleep. There is not mind or thought in sleep. Yet when one rises from sleep one says, 'I slept well'.[123]

But does such a state really exist? Ramana says that one "cannot describe that state" of realization, one "can only be that."[124] It may not be possible to describe it but it is possible to experience it:

> Pure consciousness wholly unrelated to the physical body and transcending the mind is a matter of direct experience. Sages know their bodiless, eternal existence, just as an unrealized man knows his bodily existence.[125]

PART II

CHAPTER V

SOME OTHER APPROACHES TO NORMAL EXPERIENCE

Could something else, apart from the pure subject, provide the continuity between the three states of consciousness (waking, dreaming and deep sleep)?

I

Could it be that continuity is provided by the fact that, although distinct, the three states are not entirely separate and flow into each other? For instance, the effects of the waking state on sleep (during which dreams occur) are identified with relative ease. Fatigue experienced in the waking state induces sleep. Sleep enables one to feel refreshed in the waking state.

The dream state can now be introduced as an intervening

variable. What one eats in the waking state is known to affect the quality of not just sleep but also dreams. Many a nightmare has been known to result from a bad meal. Moreover, both physical and mental events experienced in waking affect dreams. "A person dreams of his beloved woman owing to the intensity of the subconscious impression of her generated by repeated thoughts of her."[126]

Dreams, in turn, affect sleep and the waking state as well. Too many dreams, specially disturbing dreams, influence sleep; and the memory of a nightmare may continue to haunt us during the day.

Could it then be that our sense of continuity of being is derived from the fluent inter-connectedness, the confluency, of the three states? But the fact remains that the three "states alternate and differ from one another."[127] Waking is removed by sleeping, and sleeping interrupted by dreaming; dreaming is eliminated by waking up and "two entities are distinct when one can be sublated, cancelled or contradicted by the other. In other words, the sublation of one thing by another means that the former is both rejected and disvalued as a result of the experience of the latter."[128]

One must here clearly distinguish contradiction within a state from contradiction between states. Thus within the waking state we may take a thing to be something which turns out to be something else. For instance we may mistake one person for another. When the person is correctly identified the earlier impression is contradicted, but the *waking* state is not contradicted. If this kind of a misapprehension takes place in a dream, the false impression is again contradicted in the dream but the state of the dream is not contradicted. What is most striking about the three states, however, is that they contradict one another.

II

If the three states, by themselves, cannot provide the sense of continuity, could it derive from a sense of identity provided by some aspect of our personality? It is obvious that the body is present in all the three states; it is true, though less obvious, that the mind is also present in all of the three states. Could not the body or mind—or some aspect of either—therefore provide the link being sought among the three states?

The case for the *body* may be examined first. It is present in all the three states: waking, dreaming and deep sleep. Moreover, the position of the body is connected with sleep: some sleep better prone, others in a fetal position and so on. In fact the position of the body can even affect dreams. People have been awakened through nightmares when about to fall off the edge of the bedstead. The body monitors, as it were, all the three states. This is obvious in the waking state. Consider the following example in relation to the dream state: "Your alarm clock is ringing; it is five o'clock and you have to rise. The dream structure will create a dream. You are in a temple, and a bell is ringing. The alarm ringing outside has been transferred and made a part of the dream. Now the bell is ringing in the temple: now there is no need to rise. You can continue sleeping."[129] And finally, although the body recedes from consciousness in deep sleep, how would we experience deep sleep without the body and but for the body? This point is emphatically made in Buddhism when it is pointed out that even states of meditation supposedly deeper than deep sleep are experienced only in the body:

> Above this there is the *cessation of perception and feelings*, where one is said to *touch Nirvana with one's body*. Outwardly this state appears as one of coma. Motion, speech and thought are absent. Only life and warmth remain. Even the unconscious impulses are said to be *asleep*.[130]

> The highest trance is... achieved through the body. It gives great beatitude and complete calm, and since all thought is extinct, the realization of this state depends on the body. One is said "*to touch the deathless element with one's body*."[131]

The fact that consciousness in any form—including lack of it—is associated with the physical living presence of the body is undeniable. What is problematic is whether, although always found together, body and consciousness are not distinct.

The following five arguments need to be examined in this connection:

> If consciousness be a property of the body, it should be either essential to it or accidental. If the former, it should be inseparable from the body and last as long as it does; but it does not, for in a swoon or in dreamless sleep the body is seen without it. If the latter, it implies another agency at work in producing consciousness and cannot, therefore, be wholly ascribed to the body.
>
> Moreover, a person waking from a dream owns the dream experience while disowning the dream body, say that of a tiger. If the one were a property of the other, both would be avowed or disavowed together.
>
> Consciousness is always found in association with the physical organism; but it is far from certain that it ceases to be, when the organism breaks up. For aught we know, it may continue to exist in another manner; and though that such is the case is not proved, even a doubt of the kind is sufficient to reject the position that it is a property of the body.
>
> Nor can such association of the two in itself, even if constant, prove that one is a property of the other. The eye cannot see, for example, except with the aid of some kind of light; yet it cannot be said that visual perception is a property of light. Similarly in the present case also, the body may only serve as an auxiliary or condition for consciousness to manifest itself.
>
> If consciousness were really a property of the body, it would, if knowable by one, be knowable in exactly the same way by others as well. The form or complexion of our body, for instance, is perceived not only by ourselves, but also by others. A person's thoughts, feelings, dreams and memories, on the other hand, while they are immediate facts to him, are not known to any other in the same way. The knowledge which a philosopher has of his toothache is different from that of the dentist who treats it. This important difference suggests that consciousness is not a

> property of the physical body, but of something else or is itself an independent principle which only finds its medium of expression in the body.[132]

Thus although the experience of the three states of consciousness is invariably associated with the body in some form, the body cannot logically provide the essential link between the three states. Moreover, the body is itself constantly undergoing change, along with the changing mental states. It can even be argued that the body is *relatively* more stable than the mental states, in which case it can perhaps provide a relatively more continuous sense of identity. But we have overlooked one much more stable element of mental consciousness for its claim as providing the sense of identity: memory.

III

It is clear that memory provides a link during the waking state, and as we *remember* we dreamt with the dream state also, and as we *remember* we slept, with the state of deep sleep as well. Memory then is the link which ties it all together.

Recognition of personal identity is the crucial element here. In fact, over against the argument from identity through the body, the body undergoes change from childhood to youth and old age but memory is able to span this change. Hence memory is a very significant element in relation to identity. However, the *content* of memory is constantly changing so there must be some element in us which monitors the change—for not only do memories change, there is also the awareness of such change.

IV

Thus although the body and mind or elements thereof may be pressed into service to account for the fact that despite change we possess a sense of identity, the elements, themselves changing, cannot fully account for it. We know that the three states contradict one another and we know that "the psychological correlate of contradiction is an experience of discontinuity."[133] In an extreme sense every object, every memory, every experience contradicts the other. It is only the fact of the one self which holds them together, like beads on a string. They are held so tightly on the bead that the string is unseen—and we may thus "define the true self as the ultimate subject."[134]

V

The purpose of this chapter was to identify the different ways which have been devised to account for the continuity among the three basic states of consciousness. The conclusions may be summarized as follows:

(1) One manoeuvre, on the part of both the advocates of normal interpretation of ordinary experience and the advocates of the Advaitin interpretation of ordinary experience, has been to reduce the three states to two states and hence set up a binary opposition, which perhaps the human mind is either genetically programmed or structurally shaped to handle with greater ease. Advocates of the normal interpretation of ordinary experience would rather subsume dreaming within sleeping and reduce all experience to the dichotomy of waking and sleeping. The advocates of the Advaitin interpretation of ordinary experience would rather subsume waking in dreaming and reduce all experience to the dichotomy of dreaming and sleeping.

These conclusions were drawn in an earlier chapter and are being restated here for convenience. The point is, however, that whether we reduce normal experience to three, less than three, or increase it to more than three states, the problem of accounting for the continuous experience of distinct states of consciousness cannot be eliminated. All the different states as empirically experienced cannot be shown to be modifications of just one state of empirical consciousness.

(2) If this is not possible then the question arises: can one explain the fact of these states being experienced in common, though successively, in terms of only *one* agent experiencing them and can this agent be identified?

The procedure of reducing all experiences to one experiencer seems more logical than the earlier one of reducing the different states of experience somehow to just 'one' experience by devaluing the others. But the search for such a subject in the empirical realm is frustrating as neither the body nor the mind nor the two together, it would appear, succeed in meeting the criterion such a subject must meet: that as an observer of change it must itself not change.

(3) These considerations lead to the suggestion that although such a subject is the implication of all empirical experience, it is not identical with this experience. It is ever present but never seen. An illustration might help. Beads on a necklace could be placed so compactly that the underlying string could become invisible. The string then is ever present, but never seen.

(4) It is the contention of Advaita that this string can be seen—as when we take the necklace apart and put it together. And just as our perception of what a necklace is, is forever altered by this exercise, so is our perception of ourselves in a strikingly redeeming and emancipatory way, should we succeed in experiencing the ultimate subject.

(5) By its very nature the ultimate subject cannot be known in a way the ordinary things of the world are known. It can only be known through and by itself for otherwise it will not be known. If it is known the way any other object is known, it will perforce remain unknown, for it will immediately become an object of knowledge and we will be unable to know it as a subject. In *this* sense it may be called transcendental.[135]

VI

The Buddhist position in relation to the Self is very different from the Advaitin, at least on the face of it. Although there is little evidence of discussion of the three states of consciousness as such in Buddhism, there is considerable discussion of the concept of Self as such and of its relation to the body and mind in the context of the question: Is there anything underlying phenomena? First, Buddhism denies the existence of any underlying element, it "knows no being, but only becoming."[136] If now it be asked: 'How does one explain continuity of experience?', the Buddhists reply that there is no need to postulate an identity to explain continuity, and further, that continuity is self-explanatory: "When a particular idea constituting the self of a particular moment disappears, it does so after leaving its mark behind and that the self of the next moment is consequently informed by it through and through. That is, the self of a person at any instant, though not the same as it was at a previous instant, is not quite different from it."[137] And the "similarity in it is mistaken for identity"[138] by the superficial observer. Memory is explained similarly for such a self—if we may call it so—as it "is not only ... collective but also ... recollective."[139]

In the previous sections an attempt was made to examine whether the element of continuity could be identified with any element of body or mind. On this point there is an interesting comment of the Buddha that "Indeed, if any assertion can be made about a self, it would be more correct to call the body the self because, whereas the body may endure as long as a hundred years, the mind in all its forms is in constant flux, like an ape in a forest which seizes one branch only to let it go and grasp another."[140]

The orthodox Buddhist position, in opposition to the Advaitic, is that there is no 'self',[141] although the issue is clouded with considerable controversy.[142] Some Buddhists have accused non-Buddhists of foisting or somehow smuggling in the 'self' into Buddhism and would prefer being told "that the Buddha was totally wrong" in denying the Self.[143] This is what classical Advaita claims to be the case.[144] To use the words of a Buddhist scholar, "here was the weak spot in the Buddhist armour."[145] The fact that the word 'self' can have so many connotations makes the issue particularly thorny. In many of his statements Ramana is very Zen. When asked about controlling the mind he responded: "show me the mind ..."[146] "Who am I" functions as a koan.[147] And he is emphatic that the ego does not exist,[148] which brings him very close, sometimes too close, to the Buddhist position, as when he says: "...he who thinks the self is within the insentient body is like one who considers the cloth of the screen which supports a cinema picture to be contained within the picture."[149] On the Buddhist position that there is no Self, Ramana comments: "First one sees the Self as objects, then one sees the *Self as void*, and then one sees the Self as the Self; only, in this last there is no seeking because seeing is becoming."[150]

Ramana's position on this point may now be presented directly. He was asked pointedly "who is this 'I'? It seems to be only a continuum of sense-impression. The Buddhist idea seems to be so too." He replied:

> The world is not external. The impressions cannot have an outer origin. Because the world can be cognised only by consciousness. The world does not say that it exists. It is your impression. Even so this impression is not consistent and not unbroken. In deep sleep the world is not cognised; and so it exists not for a sleeping man. Therefore the world is the sequence of the ego. Find out the ego. The finding of its source is the final goal.[151]

If by Self is meant the empirical self which is part of the world and sees the world then "true spiritual experience involves the transcendence of the empirical subject in addition to the cancellation of the objective world."[152]

Could it be that the difference between Advaita and Buddhism is really heuristic? Does an image fall on the screen or does it flit across the screen? Is that area of the screen which it covers as it moves across the screen to be considered as part of the image or not? Is it simply the case that Buddhism says no in response to this question and Hinduism says yes?

CHAPTER VI

THE RECONCILIATION OF NORMAL AND ADVAITIN EXPERIENCE

In the discussion hitherto emphasis was placed on the manner in which the same spectrum of ordinary human experience, consisting of the waking, dreaming and deep sleep state, is viewed differently from what we have called the normal and the Advaitin perspective. In this chapter the discussion will be resumed and the divergence will be further examined to the point where a certain convergence will appear. Such an exercise may well help reconcile if not integrate the two perspectives on daily experience.

I

A careful survey of the discussion on the point discloses the interesting fact that there is a duality in the manner in which the three states are discussed by Advaitins, and that this duality ultimately leads to a polarity.

The duality emerges as follows. *Sometimes* the Advaitins present the three states from the vantage point of the deep sleep state. This should not come as a surprise since the Advaitins sometimes even refer to the "peak experience" of Advaita as "sleepless sleep."[153] Ramana explains:

> Enquiring further the questions arise,"Who is this 'I'? Wherefrom does it come?" 'I' was not aware in sleep. Simultaneously with its rise sleep changes to dream or wakefulness. But I am not concerned with dream just now. Who am I now, in the wakeful state? If I originated from sleep, then the 'I' was covered up with ignorance. Such an ignorant 'I' cannot be what the scriptures say or the wise ones affirm. 'I' am beyond even 'Sleep'; 'I' must be now and here and what I was all along in sleep and dreams also, without the qualities of such states. 'I' must therefore be the unqualified substratum underlying these three states.[154]

On another occasion, however, he reverses the vantage point and looks at all the three states from the standpoint of the waking state. Identifying the facts that we are *conscious* in the waking state and pure *consciousness* is our real nature he remarks: "Sometimes we forget our identities, as in sleep and dreams." Elsewhere he says:

> The ego arises when you wake up from sleep. In deep sleep you do not say that you are sleeping and that you are going to wake up or that you have been sleeping so long. But still you are there. Only when you are awake you say that you have slept. Your wakefulness comprises sleep also in it.[155]

The duality involved here consists of the fact that the features of the waking and sleeping states can be used to point to the pure subject. It is conscious. This enables it to be connected to the waking state. But it is free of subject—object duality. This enables it to be connected to the deep sleep state. This is the duality referred to above: *both* waking and sleeping may help characterize the pure subject in different ways. This is what enables the experience of the pure subject to be described in terms of "sleepless sleep."

In some other discussions, however, the duality is converted into a polarity. Ramana explains that even though sleep may in some ways be considered illustrative of the experience of the pure subject,[156] "realization is possible in faint and *impossible in sleep*."[157] Elsewhere he remarks: "Realization can only take place in the waking state."[158] This clearly contrasts with the fact that it cannot take place in sleep. Here in fact Ramana is reflecting the tendency on the part of Advaita, identified by William M. Indich, to set up two hierarchies of consciousness: a subjective one and an objective one. The subjective hierarchy proceeds from waking through dream to deep sleep. As one moves along this continuum consciousness becomes more unified: it is external in waking, internal in dreaming and neither in deep sleep and thus unified and non-dual in this sense. The objective hierarchy proceeds from deep sleep through dream to waking. There is no volition in sleep, traces of it may appear in dream but it is fully manifest in waking. *Both* approaches are required and are complementary: "The theoretical approach shows us where we want to go, i.e., to the interiorization and unification of consciousness, while the practical approach indicates the means to achieve that end, i.e., through Advaitic knowledge..."[159]

Three main points have been expounded in this chapter so far: (1) that there is complementary duality in some ways between waking and deep sleep in *characterising* the pure subject; (2) that there is a contrastive polarity between the two in *realising* the pure subject and (3) that it is possible to set up more generally what may be called subjective and objective hierarchies in terms of *formulating* all three states, rather than just waking and sleep. All these threads are brought together in Ramana's answer to the question: "*Relatively speaking*, is not sleep state nearer to pure consciousness than the waking state?"

> Yes, in this sense: When passing from sleep to waking the 'I' thought must start; the mind comes into play; thoughts arise; and then the functions of the body come into

operation; all these together make us say that we are awake. The absence of all this evolution is the characteristic of sleep and therefore it is nearer to Pure Consciousness than the waking state.

But one should not therefore desire to be always in sleep. In the first place it is impossible, for it will necessarily alternate with the other states. Secondly it cannot be the state of bliss in which the *jnani* is for his state is permanent and not alternating. Moreover, the sleep state is not recognised to be one of awareness by people; but the sage is always aware. Thus the sleep state differs from the state in which the sage is established.

Still more, the sleep state is free from thoughts and their impression to the individual. It cannot be altered by one's will because effort is impossible in that condition. Although nearer to Pure Consciousness, it is not fit for efforts to realise the Self.

The incentive to realise can arise only in the waking state and efforts can also be made only when one is awake. We learn that the thoughts in the waking state form the obstacle to gaining the stillness of sleep. "Be still and know that I am God." So stillness is the aim of the seeker. Even a single effort to still at least a single thought even for a trice goes a long way to reach the state of quiescence. Effort is required and it is possible in the waking state only. There is the effort here; there is awareness also; the thoughts are stilled; so there is the peace of sleep gained. That is the state of the *jnani*.. It is neither sleep nor waking but intermediate between the two. There is the awareness of the waking state and the stillness of sleep. Call it wakeful sleep or sleeping wakefulness or sleepless waking or wakeless sleep.[160]

II

The preceding discussion creates room for proposing a reconciliation between the normal and Advaitin analysis of daily experience. Indeed the reader may have already seen its broad outline.

The normal understanding of daily life takes the waking state as the norm because, among all the three states, this is the state in which human beings can exercise their volition to the utmost. If normal life is taken to consist of "life, liberty and the pursuit of happiness," such pursuit is most actively carried out in the waking state so long as happiness is seen to consist in the achievement of personal and professional goals in a world external to us. In a sense, therefore, our normal understanding is correct: that one can perhaps set out on a deliberately chosen course of action only in the waking state.

Advaita agrees with this pragmatic insight of normal experience. Where it differs is in redefining the *goal* of this activity as the realization of the pure subject. It identifies this goal in a fresh philosophical analysis of the three states as pointing to the pure subject, but any movement towards that goal must commence, like all activities, in the waking state. Even those who recognize the role of dreams in human living point out, for instance, that "our conscious minds are needed if we are to make the most of our dreams; *by bringing them into waking consciousness* and learning to understand them we may be led to a reappraisal of our whole mode of being."[161] Very broadly one might say that the normal and Advaitin analyses coincide in terms of what has been called the 'objective' hierarchy but differ in terms of the subjective hierarchy.

III

There is, therefore, between the normal and Advaitin analyses this general convergence on the point that the exercise of volition presupposes the waking state. But although the two might start out from the same point they start moving in different directions almost at once. This becomes obvious when we consider what may be called the phenomenon of consciousness—compression. Normal consciousness tends to compress *sleeping and dreaming* together into more or less one state so that the trichotomy of waking, dreaming and deep sleep is reduced to the two levels of waking and sleeping. Advaitin analysis does the opposite and tries to compress *waking and dreaming* into one and reduce the trichotomy to a dichotomy of dreaming and sleeping. The difference is accounted for by distinct concepts of consciousness.

The normal view of daily living invariably associates consciousness with consciousness of objects. These objects become murky in dreaming and disappear in deep sleep. Thus the only effective domain of consciousness is reduced to the waking state—and the rest can be lumped together as lacking in intrinsic significance. "According to this view, the experiences we call dreams are no more than glimpses of this material running through our sleeping brains as they carry out their nightly operation of 'information processing.' It has even been suggested that the stories of our dreams are inventions of the waking mind, which attempts to impose some kind of sense and order on the isolated pieces of information being processed and bind them into a meaningful whole. And finally, it is maintained that even to awaken accidentally during sleep is to interrupt a vital process which would be better left undisturbed from the point of view of our mental efficiency. Dreaming is believed to be the actual information-processing activity, and the purpose of sleep to allow this to take place. If we are deprived of the opportunity to 'dream,' say the computer theorists, we must eventually break down because the brain's existing programs are not being up-dated in the light of new information. This must necessarily result in maladaptive, neurotic behaviour."[162]

It is natural, then, that one would also use the waking state as the criterion for the reality of consciousness when consciousness is meant to invariably imply consciousness of objects. Thus, if one is in doubt as to whether one is dreaming or thinking, one may conclude that "one must have been dreaming, not thinking, as the events of the 'dream' are unreal and inconsistent with the facts of everyday life."[163]

The Advaitic view veers in a different direction and tends to equate waking and dreaming. On the face of it, however, waking and dreaming appear quite distinct and there are perhaps even good reasons for maintaining this distinction.

The fact that "in the waking state the dream is determined to be *false*, whereas in the dream the waking state is not so determined" and the further fact that we can *recall* dream experiences in the waking state but cannot recall waking state experiences in a dream (even if waking and dream state experiences influence each other) are two of the strongest arguments in favour of establishing the primacy of the waking state over the dream state. Not only has Advaita had to face these arguments quite often, they are also of long standing.[164] What answers does it have to offer and how convincing are they?

Let us refer to the first argument as the argument by *falsity* and to the second as the argument by *memory*.

Several points are urged against the argument by falsity. One of them is to maintain that *both* dream and waking share the characteristics of purposefulness and permanency and *both* are unreal. This is clearly the thrust of the following passage:

> 138-44. "The difference between dreams and the wakeful state lies in the fact that in the waking state the dream is determined to be false, whereas in the dream the waking state is not so determined. Therefore the waking state is universally taken to be real. But this is wrong. For do you not experience the same extent of permanency and purposefulness in dreams as in the wakeful state?
>
> "Wakeful consciousness does not intervene in dreams nor does dream-consciousness intervene in the wakeful state, while the two factors—enduring nature and purposefulness—are common to both.
>
> "Examine your past dreams and past waking experiences in the light of these facts and see for yourself.
>
> "Again, note the appearance of reality in magical phenomena and the seeming purposeful actions of magical creations. Does reality rest on the slender basis of such appearances?
>
> "The confusion is due to want of discrimination between

> the real and the unreal among ignorant folk. Ignorantly indeed do they say that the wakeful universe is real.[165]

If it be argued that nevertheless the waking state *contradicts* dream then two other lines of argument open up. One is that in this case each state can be said to contradict the other; thus dreaming contradicts waking as much as waking contradicts sleep. The other is to argue that contradiction per se does not constitute proof of unreality.

> "I shall now tell you briefly the difference between reality and unreality.
>
> "Reality is that whose existence is self-evident and does not require other aids to reveal it. Unreality is the contrary.
>
> (149) "If you say, however, that a thing is real until and unless its existence is contradicted, consider the example of a coil of rope being mistaken for a snake. The fancied snake would according to you be *real* in the interval antecedent to correct knowledge but that is absurd.
>
> (150-151)"Furthermore, if contradiction means non-existence, the mental image of the thing contradicted must be admitted, and that means the thing verbally denied is mentally admitted. Therefore contradiction leads one nowhere and does not determine the unreality of a thing; nor does the appearance of a thing determine its reality. Appearance and contradiction are both intermediate.[166]

However, it could still be argued that *contradicting* knowledge is more true or real than *contradicted* knowledge and "since dream experience is contradicted by waking experience [the latter] is relatively more real."[167]

One must now explore the nature of contradiction. "There are two kinds of contradiction, experiential and logical. The perception of an existence as a snake is contradicted by a stronger or better perception of it as a rope. Actual experience is here corrected by another actual experience. We have here experiential contradiction. This is what is ordinarily and almost universally regarded as the mark of unreality. Sankara also admits this. But he (like some thinkers of the West, e.g. Zeno, Kant and

Bradley) also recognizes a kind of logical contradiction which consists in actual experience being proved inconsistent by thought, or one thought being contradicted by another thought."[168]

Although *experientially* the waking state contradicts dreaming and the opposite does not happen, there is another aspect of dreams that leads to a logical contradiction: the fact that the *actual* content of dreams is supplied, at least at times, by the waking state, while dreams are only normally *recalled* or remembered in waking and do not form its direct content.

> Since the experience of dream is like that of waking, the latter is considered to be the cause of dream. Now, dream which is the effect is illusory; and it must logically follow that waking, the cause, is of the same nature as the effect. It is only to the dreamer, i.e., to the one who is under the spell of illusion that waking appears to be real. In the state of waking one sees what is unreal, and being absorbed in it, sees the same in dream also. In dream too one sees what is unreal, but on waking does not see it. The state of waking is said to be the cause of dream only in the sense that to it may be traced the contents of dream. There is no absolute causality for waking. In both the states what is seen is unreal.[169]

Thus while by the logic of experience in the waking state, dream is determined to be false and not vice versa, by the experience of logic in the waking state, *the waking state* can be determined to be false, whereas in the dream state dream cannot be determined to be false in the same way.

One may now turn to the argument by memory. The basic point here is that we can *remember* dreams in the waking state but not waking states in dream. It will help to begin with the initial observation that out of two experiences, *only* the shorter can be recalled in the longer one. This argument can be considered on two levels. As "dream creations are transitory in relation to the waking state," one cannot recall the waking state in dream just as one cannot recall in two minutes of a wedding ceremony the two hour long wedding ceremony.

But, it might be objected, a ceremony of two hours can be recalled in two minutes *after* it is over. But this then is the next level at which the argument operates. Dreaming is never over until deep sleep. The point needs to be understood carefully. It is indeed possible to recall a day's events in two minutes after the day is over; the next day, for example. It is not possible, however, to recall *during* the day itself the events of the day within any two minutes constitutive of it, because the two minutes are part of the day itself. This shows that we cannot recall *the waking state within the dreaming because it is a part of the dreaming itself.* When the dreaming, like the day, is over, as represented by deep sleep, we can recall the whole dream, including its waking-segment, in a minute! In other words, after deep sleep we can recall *both* what happened during dreaming and during waking, both of which were parts of it and contained within it. This is confirmed by the fact that when we are awakened directly from dreaming we can recall both the dream and the waking state which preceded it, which is really part of it.

IV

Neither normal nor Advaitin analysis, however, can quite dispense with the three state analysis. In the case of normal analysis of daily life even after the interaction of dreaming and waking,[170] and the fact that dreaming takes place in sleep are accounted for,[171] the independent status of dream as a state of consciousness cannot be gainsaid. In the phenomenon of lucid dream for instance "*the dreamer is aware at the time of dreaming that he is dreaming,* and feels himself to be in possession of what we call normal waking consciousness while knowing himself quite certainly to be asleep in bed."[172] Moreover, at least in the case of certain dreams it has been plausibly asked: "why should not our dream life, like our waking life, contain experiences that are ends in themselves...?"[173] In the case of Advaita, for instance, *even if* waking is considered a form of dreaming, it is in this state alone that realization can take place. This is clear from the following exchange of Ramana:

Q. How is realization made possible?

A. There is the absolute Self from which a spark proceeds as from fire. The spark is called EGO. In the case of the ignorant it identifies itself with some object simultaneously with its rise. It cannot remain independent of such association. This association is ignorance whose destruction is the object of our efforts. If ego's objectifying tendency is killed it remains pure and also merges in its source. We can separate ourselves from that which is external but not from that which is one with us. Hence ego is not one with body. *This must be realised in the waking state.*[174]

In fact one could speak of "lucid sleep" by analogy with "lucid dream." Just as lucid dream consists of waking awareness while dreaming, lucid sleep would consist of waking awareness while sleeping—"in deep sleep state we lay down our ego ... our thoughts and our desires. If we could only do all this while we are conscious, we would realize the self."[175]

CHAPTER VII

ADVAITIN EXPERIENCE IN THE COURSE OF DAILY LIVING

I

How is this pure subject to be known or experienced?

One must begin by examining the use of the 'words' "knowledge" and "experience" in the context of the pure subject. It would be apparent from what has been said that these words cannot be applied to the pure subject in their accepted usage. When we say that we know something—as when I say that I know you are reading this book—the concept of knowledge involves a knower, namely, "I", and a known, namely, "You." Knowledge then constitutes a relationship between the two. In other words, knowledge as we know it in normal experience invariably involves a dichotomy between the knower and the known. The same is also true of the word 'experience' in its normal connotation. If reading this book turns out to be an interesting experience, then immediately a duality is involved;

that of the experiencer and the experienced. It is clear, then, that in their ordinary acceptation, *knowledge* and *experience* both presuppose a distinction between the knower and the known and the experiencer and the experienced; that is, between subject and object.

But is it invariably so? There are at least two statements we often make in the course of daily living which seem to constitute, at least at first sight, an exception to what has been said above. One of them is the statement: "I know myself" or "As you yourself know..." and the second is the statement, "I slept last night." In the case of "I know myself"—the knower and the known are the same *I myself*. Here the same entity, "I" is both the subject *and* object of knowledge. However, it will be obvious on a little reflection that in this case the "I" itself has been divided into two: "the knowing I" and the "the known I." The question at issue is: not how do 'I' know 'I' but how do I know the "*knowing I*?" The moment I claim to know the *knowing I*, the *knowing I* has become the *known I* and the process of infinitesimal subdivision sets in, with no end in sight. Hence the statement "I know myself" constitutes a limitation to which even self-knowledge as ordinarily understood, is subject. It does not constitute an exception, only a limitation.

The second statement: "I slept last night" is of interest because in the actual experience of sleep the distinction between the subject and the object disappears. In sleep *we* are not aware that we are asleep, in contrast to the statement "I know myself" which is made in a state in which and of which we are aware. The curiosity in terms of the experience of sleep lies in the fact that one can never refer to it *in the present*. One can say "I will sleep" (future) or that "I slept" (past). One cannot say "I am asleep" for the very statement constitutes a denial of that claim as one cannot *consciously* talk when asleep.

Thus when the expressions 'knowledge' and 'experience' are ordinarily used, they invariably involve a distinction between subject and object. It is true that we also use these terms to refer to some experience in which the dichotomy seems to dissolve or at least becomes questionable, as in the case of knowing oneself and experiencing sleep. Yet when these cases are closely examined, they constitute limitations rather than exceptions, caused in one case by the *atomicity* which the subject is capable of achieving as a subject of knowledge, and in the other case, by the density which an experience like sleep involves, in which the subject and object both merge.

A few comments will clarify the point further. Whenever we do refer to the experience of sleep it is when we are *out* of that state, for when we are out of that state, it can be made an object of knowledge or experience. In sleep not only can one not say "I am asleep" 'one also cannot say' "I know myself" because *any* split between subject and object—even within the subject—is not possible. In fact, when even in the waking state we say "I know myself," it is only a case of partial knowledge—for we know the known self, not the *knowing* self. When one is so deeply immersed in thought that the thinker and the thought have virtually merged, it is not possible to say "I am thinking." It is only after the thinking process has descended to a level where the two are sufficiently disengaged that one can say "I am thinking."

Thus, *strictly speaking*, the words 'knowledge' and 'experience' cannot be applied to the "pure subject". But they are indeed so applied. They are so applied because of the poverty of language—because the use of language itself involves a division into subject and object. This incongruity could well be the reason why silence has acquired such a profound connotation in some religious traditions. When these expressions are applied to the pure subject, when we talk of knowing or experiencing the pure subject, it is to be understood in the way we talk of experiencing sleep. It applies to not *when* one is asleep but *before* or *after* the event, when the actual experience can be objectified—when the subject-object division has reappeared.

Another verbal strategy could be adopted. Instead of stating that the words *knowing* and *experience* are to be understood in a *special* sense on the analogy of sleep in the context of pure subject, one could abandon these words and save the word *realize* for the special kind of knowledge involved here. This may not be possible as language is not our private property, but the suggestion enables one to develop the theme further. For even the use of the word *realize* poses a problem. To *realize* literally means 'to make real!' Now presumably what is made real was in some sense previously not real, otherwise to *realize* would not make much sense. It has already been demonstrated that the pure subject is *always* present and in that sense always real, and hence cannot be made real as it always is real. In another sense, though, one may speak of realization; that is, in the sense of realizing as existent what always existed anyway. The point which emerges is that although we will be using words like 'know', 'experience' or 'realize', they are to be understood in the context of the pure subject with great circumspection.

II

If we accept as a concession to popular, and even empirical, usage that words like 'knowing' or 'experiencing' or 'realizing' may be applied to gaining access to the pure subject, the question remains: how does one come to know, experience or realize it?

The answer offered to this question in Advaita is, on the face of it, rather puzzling and perhaps even off-putting. One is told that one knows, experiences or realizes it *by being it* or *becoming it*!! In terms of normal linguistic usage this can be made to appear odd, even bizarre. Do I know a table by becoming it? Do I experience a meal by becoming it? Do I experience my friend's deception by becoming it? The case seems rather to the contrary. I know a table by remaining distinct from it, a meal by eating it, and come to know of my friend's deception by being a victim of it.

There are, however, other kinds of experience in the context of which the expression makes much more sense. If I wanted to know what it means to be an athlete or even a student the best way of doing so is perhaps indeed to become one. Similarly, one really comes to know what it means to be a bachelor by remaining one or what it means to be married by, well, marrying! One knows what it means to be a father by being or by becoming a father; one knows what it means to be a wife by becoming a wife, a mother by becoming a mother, a child by being a child. Thus when we move from knowing an 'object in existence' to knowing a 'state of existence', the Advaitic statement that one knows something by being it or becoming it somehow starts sounding less absurd. Or to put it another way, as one switches from objective knowledge to subjective knowledge the Advaitic dictum begins to sound more credible.

Let us then examine the realm of subjective experience a little more closely. All the examples of subjective experience such as fatherhood, motherhood, etc., mentioned above share one feature in common: they are attributes which apply to a person and the person retains the sense of personhood independently of the attribute. Thus a person may be a father or a mother. A person who wants to know what it means to be a father may do so by becoming a father. The person, however, does not thereby lose his personhood in the process of acquiring fatherhood. There is, however, at least one form of subjective experience in order to *gain* which one must *lose* one's sense of personhood. In order to experience sleep, for instance, one must forego one's individual identity. So long as one retains one's individual identity, one cannot sleep; so long as one is asleep one cannot recover one's individual identity. The identity can be recovered on waking up—but then sleep vanishes, though not the memory thereof. But being actually asleep and knowing one has slept are two different things, actually two different experiences.

Now if one were asked: "How do I come to know what sleep is?", the proper answer would seem to be, "By sleeping". Let us now analyze what is involved in sleeping. What happens when one sleeps? One could plausibly answer with any of the following responses: that one is overcome by sleep, or that one becomes one with sleep or that one gets absorbed in sleep or lost in sleep. Another more dramatic answer could be: *one becomes sleep*. And why is it possible to say so? It is possible to say so because *within sleep there are no distinctions of any kind*.

One is now well situated, I would think, to understand the purport of the following remarks of Ramana:

> Knowing the Self means being the Self. Can you say that you do not know the Self? Though you cannot see your own eyes and though not provided with a mirror to look in, do you deny the existence of your eyes? Similarly, you are aware of the Self even though the Self is not objectified. Or, do you deny your Self because it is not objectified? When you say 'I cannot know the Self,' it means absence in

> terms of relative knowledge, because you have been so accustomed to relative knowledge that you identify yourself with it. Such wrong identity has forged the difficulty of not knowing the obvious Self because it cannot be objectified. And then you ask 'how is one to know the Self?'[176]

III

Notwithstanding the jibe in the last sentence of the preceding quotation, the time is now ripe to ask the crucial question: how does one become, or, if you wish, become one with the pure subject?

One point is immediately clear—that it must involve a process of withdrawal and introspection. This may be established both analogically and logically. The analogy of sleep is again helpful here. If one wishes to become one *with* sleep, one withdraws the mind *from* everything else. One chooses a quiet place or a serene atmosphere so as to prevent the mind from getting *extroverted* by high-decibel sounds, high-voltage lights and so on. In fact to become one with anything—or to concentrate on any *one* thing—one must withdraw the mind from *all* those other things which will draw it away from the one thing the mind wants to identify with, be it a book, a T.V. show or one's pet hobby.

This point can be presented even more sharply in logical terms. For if one wishes to unite with the subject which is one's Self—one must travel within, just as one must turn one's attention without if one wishes to 'become one with' external objects. Ramana is quite explicit on this point: "How can one make the Quest, 'who am I'? The way is subjective, not objective; so it cannot and need not be shown by another. Is it necessary to show anyone the way inside his own house? If the seeker keeps his mind still, that will be enough."[177] Elsewhere he writes: "Who sees stones? They are perceived by your mind. So they are in your mind. Whose mind is it? The questioner must find himself. If the Self be found, this question would not arise. The Self is more intimate than objects. Find the subject and the objects will take care of themselves. The objects are seen by different persons, according to their outlook and theories are evolved. But who is the seer?, the recognizer of these theories? It is you. Find your Self. Then there is an end of these vagaries of the mind."[178]

The search for the pure subject, therefore, is a quest within oneself. It is otherwise known as self-inquiry. This method is not unknown to ancient Advaita but was refined into a definite technique by Ramana Maharshi. The technique is summarized below:

> Beginners in self-enquiry were advised by Sri Ramana to put their attention on the inner feeling of 'I' and to hold that feeling as long as possible. They would be told that if their attention was distracted by other thoughts they should revert to awareness of the 'I'-thought whenever they became aware that their attention had wandered. He suggested various aids to assist this process—one could ask oneself 'Who am I?' or 'Where does this I come from?'—but the ultimate aim was to be continuously aware of the 'I' which assumes that it is responsible for all the activities of the body and the mind.
>
> In the early stages of practice attention to the feeling 'I' is a mental activity which takes the form of a thought or a perception. As the practice develops the thought 'I' gives way to a subjectively experienced feeling of 'I', and when this feeling ceases to connect and identify with thoughts and objects it completely vanishes. What remains is an experience of being in which the sense of individuality has temporarily ceased to operate. The experience may be intermittent at first but with repeated practice it becomes easier and easier to reach and maintain. When self-enquiry reaches this level there is an effortless awareness of being in which individual effort is no longer possible since the 'I' who makes the effort has temporarily ceased to exist. It is not Self-realization since the 'I'-thought periodically reasserts itself but it is the highest level of practice. Repeated experience of this state of being weakens and destroys the mental tendencies which cause the 'I'-thought to rise, and, when their hold has been sufficiently weakened, the power

> of the Self destroys the residual tendencies so completely that the 'I'-thought never rises again. This is the final and irreversible state of Self realization.[179]

There are powerfully concise formulations of the method offered by Ramana himself. On January 23, 1937 he declared, with binary brevity, that the teachings under discussion here are contained in the two biblical statements:

> "I am that I AM" and "Be still and know that I am God."[180]

He unpacked the statements thus:

> "Be still and know that I am God." Here stillness is total surrender without a vestige of ego. Stillness will prevail and there will be no agitation of mind. Agitation of mind is the cause of desire, the sense of doership, personality. If that is stopped there is quiet. There 'Knowing' means 'Being.' It is not relative knowledge involving the triads. "I am that I am." "I am" is God—not thinking "I am God." Realise "I am" and do not *think* I am. "Know I am God"—it is said, and not "Think I am God." Your duty is TO BE, and not to be this or that. "I AM THAT I AM" sums up the whole truth; the method is summarised in BE STILL. And what does Stillness mean? It means 'Destroy yourself;' because every name and form is the cause of trouble.[181]

IV

What happens when the pure subject is experienced?

This question is bound to arise sooner or later, and perhaps sooner rather than later, in the reader's mind. It is likely to arise out of a natural curiosity; moreover, out of a natural curiosity abetted by the experiential orientation of Advaita in general and this presentation in particular. I think the question is best answered by those who are believed to have had the experience itself. Some of these accounts are contained in the next chapter. The larger issue of the relationship of these experiences to the normal experience of daily living has already been discussed in Chapter Four.

It is worth noting, however, that although the experience of the pure subject eludes us in the course of normal living, our daily life is not entirely devoid of glimpses of it. Ramana says for instance:

> The ego in its purity is experienced in the intervals between two states or between two thoughts.[182]

It is clear from other references that the states refer here to the three states of waking, dreaming and deep sleep. Ramana identifies one moment in our daily life in which, more frequently than any other, we come closest to experiencing the pure subject:

> At the time of waking up and before one actually becomes fully aware of the external world, that interval, timeless, spaceless, is the state of the true I.[183]

> Just awaking from sleep and before becoming aware of the world, there is that pure 'I'—'I'. Hold to it without sleeping or without allowing thoughts to possess you. If that is held firm it does not matter even though the world is seen. The seer remains unaffected by the phenomena.[184]

Perhaps by learning to wake up every day à la Ramana one day we will Wake Up! "Just before waking up from sleep, there is a very brief state, free from thought. That should be made permanent."[185]

The preceding comment suggests another approach to the Advaitin experience in the course of daily living. The obscuration of the pure subject can be discussed in terms of the three states of consciousness, but it can also be discussed in terms of a phenomenon characteristic of all of them: *the flow of thoughts*.

> What is meditation? It consists in expulsion of thoughts. All the present troubles are due to thoughts and are themselves thoughts. Give up thoughts. That is happiness, and also meditation. The thoughts are for the thinker. Remain as the Self of the thinker and there is an end of thoughts.[186]

Two operations are involved here: (1) the recognition that all daily living is characterised by a flow of thoughts or mental activity in some form and (2) that the cessation of this flow comprises realization. Both points need to be explored further.

The waking state is characterised by a continuous flow of thoughts; so is the dreaming state. What about deep sleep? Unless there was a thought-flow continuing through it we should wake up from deep sleep severed of our past. The fact that we can *remember* having slept, or *know* that we were unconscious establishes a flow of thoughts—howsoever tranquil—in that state as well.

Hence to say that a veil of thoughts conceals the pure subject or that the three states render it invisible are convertible statements. The Advaitic problem can be rephrased thus: how is the veil rent? How is one to arrest or at least interrupt this flow? This is tantamount to saying: "find out the underlying reality behind these states."

This emphasis on cessation of thoughts is not new with Ramana. An early text states:

> "Though [one] ..... be well grounded in the theory and the discussion of the philosophy of the Self, he cannot realise the Self because it is not *realisable* but already *realised*. Realization is not attained by going far, but only by staying still, not by thought (intellection) but by cessation of thought.
>
> *****
>
> Therefore it was also said that the sole necessity for Self-Realization is purity of mind. The only impurity of the mind is thought. To make it thought-free is to keep it pure.[188]

The *methods* suggested by Ramana are said to possess elements of novelty.[189]

> Q: How should a beginner start this practice ?
>
> A: The mind will subside only by means of the enquiry 'Who am I?' The thought 'Who am I?', destroying all other thoughts, will itself finally be destroyed like the stick used for stirring the funeral pyre. If other

thoughts rise, one should, without attempting to complete them, enquire 'To whom did they rise?' What does it matter however many thoughts rise? At the very moment that each thought rises, if one vigilantly enquires 'To whom did this rise?', it will be known 'To me.' If one then enquires 'Who am I?', the mind will turn back to its source [the Self] and the thought which had risen will also subside. By repeatedly practising thus, the power of the mind to abide in its source increases.

....Just as a pearl diver, tying a stone to his waist, dives into the sea and takes the pearl lying at the bottom, so everyone, diving deep within himself with non-attachment, can attain the pearl of Self. If one resorts uninterruptedly to remembrance of one's real nature [*swarupa-smarana*] until one attains Self, that alone will be sufficient...[190]

Q: You say one can realise the Self by a search for it. What is the character of this search ?

A: You are the mind or think that you are the mind. The mind is nothing but thoughts. Now behind every particular thought there is a general thought which is the 'I', that is yourself. Let us call this 'I' the first thought. Stick to this 'I'-thought and question it to find out what it is. When this question takes strong hold on you, you cannot think of other thoughts.

Q: When I do this and cling to myself, that is, the 'I'—thought, other thoughts come and go, but I say to myself 'Who am I?' and there is no answer forthcoming. To be in this condition is the practice. Is it so?

A: This is a mistake that people often make. What happens when you make a serious quest for the Self is that the 'I'-thought disappears and something else from the depths takes hold of you and that is not the 'I' which commenced the quest.

Q: What is this something else?

A: That is the real Self, the import of 'I'. It is not the ego. It is the supreme being itself.

Q: But you have often said that one must reject other thoughts when one begins the quest but the thoughts are endless. If one thought is rejected, another comes and there seems to be no end at all.

A: I do not say that you must go on rejecting thoughts. Cling to yourself, that is, to the 'I'-thought. When your interest keeps you to that single idea, other thoughts will automatically get rejected and they will vanish.[191]

V

One final point. The investigation into "Who am I" or "Whence am I" or "To whom do thoughts arise" is not intended as a meditation to be pursued *outside* the course of one's daily living, either during a meditation-time set apart for it or by retiring from the world and becoming a monk. It is meant to be practised in the course of daily living.[192]

Q. How can my mind be still if I have to use it more than other people? I want to go into solitude and renounce my headmaster's work.

A. No. You may remain where you are and go on with work. What is the undercurrent which vivifies the mind, enables it to do all this work? Why, the Self! So, that is the real source of your activity. Simply become aware of it during your work and do not forget it. Contemplate in the background of your mind even whilst working. To do that, DO NOT HURRY. Take your own time; keep the remembrance of real nature alive, even whilst working, and avoid haste which causes you to forget. Be deliberate. Practise meditation to still the mind and cause it to become aware of its true relationship to the Self, which supports it. (He gave simile, spoke of a wheel, whether thin or thick, all within the same circle, so intellect-work is within the same circle of Self). Do not imagine it is you who are doing the work. Think that it is the underlying current which is doing it. Identify yourself with this current. If you work unhurriedly, recollectedly, your work or service need not be a hindrance.[193]

CHAPTER VIII

SOME ACCOUNTS OF ADVAITIN EXPERIENCE

In this chapter the Advaitin experience as narrated by those who have had it, namely the experience of pure subject or pure consciousness, will be presented. Three such accounts—those of Ramana, of his 'disciple' Paul Brunton and of Nisargadatta—have been selected for presentation.

I
THE EXPERIENCE OF RAMANA

The incident is said to have taken place in the middle of 1896 when Ramana was in his seventeenth year. "Long after this event, he was often queried by his devotees as to how he was transformed and the following is substantially what he himself said; substantially but not literally. The author explains: "The exact words have not been recorded. The Swami as a rule talks quite impersonally. There is seldom any clear or pronounced reference to 'I' or 'you' in what he says. The genius of Tamil is specially suited for such impersonal utterances, and he generally talks Tamil. However, one studying his words and ways discovers personal references, mostly veiled. His actual words may be found too colourless and hazy to suit or appeal to many readers, especially of the Western type. Hence the use here of the customary phraseology with its distinct personal reference."[194] With this rider in mind one may now turn to the account itself.

> It was about six weeks before I left Madurai for good that the great change in my life took place. It was so sudden. One day I sat up alone on the first floor of my uncle's house. I was in my usual health. I seldom had any illness. I was a heavy sleeper. When I was at Dindigul in 1891 a huge crowd had gathered close to the room where I slept and tried to rouse me by shouting and knocking at the door, all in vain, and it was only by their getting into my room and giving me a violent shake that I was roused from my torpor. This heavy sleep was rather a proof of good health. I was also subject to fits of half-awake sleep at night. My wily playmates, afraid to trifle with me when I was awake, would go to me when I was asleep, rouse me, take me all round the playground, beat me, cuff me, sport with me, and bring me back to my bed—and all the while I would put up with everything with a meekness, humility, forgiveness, and passivity unknown to my waking state. When the morning broke I had no remembrance of the night's experiences. But these fits did not render me weaker or less fit for life and were hardly to be considered a disease. So, on that day as I sat alone there was nothing wrong with my health. But a sudden and unmistakable fear of death seized me. I felt I was going to die. Why I should have so felt cannot now be explained by anything felt in my body. Nor could I explain it to myself then. I did not however trouble myself to discover if the fear was well grounded. I felt 'I was going to die,' and at once set about thinking out what I should do. I did not care to consult

doctors or elders or even friends. I felt I had to solve the problem myself then and there.

The shock of fear of death made me at once introspective, or 'introverted.' I said to myself mentally, i.e., without uttering the words—'Now, death has come. What does it mean? What is it that is dying? This body dies.' I at once dramatized the scene of death. I extended my limbs and held them rigid as though *rigor-mortis* had set in. I imitated a corpse to lend an air of reality to my further investigation, I held my breath and kept my mouth closed, pressing the lips tightly together so that no sound might escape. Let not the word 'I' or any other word be uttered! 'Well then,' said I to myself, 'this body is dead. It will be carried stiff to the burning ground and there burnt and reduced to ashes. But with the death of this body, am "I" dead? Is the body "I"? This body is silent and inert. But I feel the full force of my personality and even the sound "I" within myself,—apart from the body. So "I" am a spirit, a thing transcending the body. The material body dies, but the spirit transcending it cannot be touched by death. I am therefore the deathless spirit.' All this was not a mere intellectual process, but flashed before me vividly as living truth, something which I perceived immediately, without any argument almost. 'I' was something very real, the only real thing in that state, and all the conscious activity that was connected with my body was centred on that. The 'I' or my 'self' was holding the focus of attention by a powerful fascination from that time forwards. Fear of death had vanished at once and forever. Absorption in the self has continued from that moment right up to this time. Other thoughts may come and go like the various notes of a musician, but the 'I' continues like the basic or fundamental *sruti* note which accompanies and blends with all other notes. Whether the body was engaged in talking, reading or anything else, I was still centred on 'I'. Previous to that crisis I had no clear perception of myself and was not consciously attracted to it. I had felt no direct perceptible interest in it, much less any permanent disposition to dwell upon it. The consequences of this new habit were soon noticed in my life.[195]

Paul Brunton has also offered a brief account of this experience based on Ramana's reminiscing:

> Maharshi told once how he got realization. On the day his father died he felt puzzled by death and pondered over it, whilst his mother and brothers wept. He thought for hours and after the corpse was cremated he got by analysis to the point of perceiving that it was the 'I' which makes the body to see, to run, to walk and to eat. "I now know this 'I' but my father's 'I' has left the body."[196]

This experience induced by the loss of his father took place in 1892, four years prior to the incident detailed earlier.

II
THE EXPERIENCE OF PAUL BRUNTON

Paul Brunton, a successful English journalist, "started out to India in 1930 in quest of the unknown truth behind all life"[197] and by his own account as contained in his book, *A Search in Secret India*,[198] discovered it in the presence of Maharshi. What follows is an account of his experience in his own words.

> My pen would wander on into some account of the scenic life around me, and into further record of many talks with the Maharishee, but it is now time to draw this chronicle to a close.
>
> I study him intently and gradually come to see in him the child of a remote Past, when the discovery of spiritual truth was reckoned of no less value than is the discovery of a gold mine today. It dawns upon me with increasing force that in this quiet and obscure corner of South India, I have been led to one of the last of India's spiritual supermen. The serene figure of this living sage brings the legendary figures of his country's ancient Rishees nearer to me. One senses that the most wonderful part of this man is withheld. His deepest soul, which one instinctively recognizes as being loaded with rich wisdom, eludes one.

At times he still remains curiously aloof, and at other times the kindly benediction of his interior grace binds me to him with hoops of steel. I learn to submit to the enigma of his personality, and to accept him as I find him. But if, humanly speaking, he is well insulated against outside contacts, whoever discovers the requisite Ariadne's thread can walk the inner path leading to spiritual contact with him. And I like him greatly because he is so simple and modest, when an atmosphere of authentic greatness lies so palpably around him; because he makes no claims to occult powers and hierophantic knowledge to impress the mystery-loving nature of his countrymen; and because he is so totally without any traces of pretension that he strongly resists every effort to canonize him during his lifetime.

It seems to me that the presence of men like the Maharishee ensures the continuity down history of a divine message from regions not easily accessible to us all. It seems to me, further, that one must accept the fact that such a sage comes to reveal something to us, not to argue anything with us. At any rate, his teachings make a strong appeal to me for his personal attitude and practical method, when understood, are quite scientific in their way. He brings in no supernatural power and demands no blind religious faith. The sublime spirituality of the Maharishee's atmosphere and the rational self-questioning of his philosophy find but a faint echo in yonder temple. Even the word "God" is rarely on his lips. He avoids the dark and debatable waters of wizardry, in which so many promising voyages have ended in shipwreck. He simply puts forward a way of self-analysis, which can be practised irrespective of any ancient or modern theories and beliefs which one may hold, a way that will finally lead man to true self-understanding.

I follow this process of self-divestment in the effort to arrive at pure integral being. Again and again I am aware that the Maharishee's mind is imparting something to my own, though no words may be passing between us. The shadow of impending departure hangs over my efforts, yet I spin out my stay until bad health takes a renewed hand in the game and accelerates an irrevocable decision to go. Indeed, out of the deep inner urgency which drew me here, has come enough will power to overthrow the plaints of a tired sick body and a weary brain and to enable me to maintain residence in this hot static air. But Nature will not be defeated for long and before long a physical breakdown becomes threateningly imminent. Spiritually my life is nearing its peak, but—strange paradox!—physically it is slipping downwards to a point lower than it has hitherto touched. For a few hours before the arrival of the culminating experience of my contact with the Maharishee, I start to shiver violently and to perspire with abnormal profuseness—intimations of coming fever.

I return hastily from an exploration of some usually veiled sanctuaries of the great temple and enter the hall when the evening meditation period has run out half its life. I slip quietly to the floor and straightaway assume my regular meditation posture. In a few seconds I compose myself and bring all wandering thoughts to a strong centre. An intense interiorization of consciousness comes with the closing of eyes.

The Maharishee's seated form floats in a vivid manner before my mind's eye. Following his frequently repeated instruction I endeavour to pierce through the mental picture into that which is formless, his real being and inner nature, his soul. To my surprise the effort meets with almost instantaneous success and the picture disappears again, leaving me with nothing more than a strongly felt sense of his intimate presence.

The mental questionings which have marked most of my earlier meditations have lately begun to cease. I have repeatedly interrogated my consciousness of physical, emotional and mental sensations in turn, but, dissatisfied in the quest of self, have eventually left them all. I have then applied the attention of consciousness to its own centre, striving to become aware of its place of origin. Now comes the supreme moment. In that concentration of stillness, the mind withdrawn into itself, one's familiar world begins to fade off into shadowy vagueness. One is apparently environed for a while by sheer nothingness, having arrived at a kind of mental blank wall. And one has to be as intense as possible to maintain one's fixed attention. But how hard to leave the lazy dalliance of our surface life and draw the mind inwards to a pin-point of concentration!

Tonight I flash swiftly to this point, with barely a skirmish against the continuous sequence of thoughts which usually play the prelude to its arrival. Some new and powerful force comes into dynamic action within my inner world and bears me inwards with resistless speed. The first great battle is over, almost without a stroke, and a pleasurable, happy, easeful feeling succeeds its high tension.

In the next stage I stand apart from the intellect, conscious that it is thinking, but warned by an intuitive voice that it is merely an instrument. I watch these thoughts with a weird detachment. The power to think, which has hitherto been a matter for merely ordinary pride, now becomes a thing from which to escape, for I perceive with startling clarity that I have been its unconscious captive. There follows the sudden desire to stand outside the intellect and just *be*. I want to dive into a place deeper than thought. I want to know what it will feel like to deliver myself from the constant bondage of the brain, but to do so with all my attention awake and alert.

It is strange enough to be able to stand aside and watch the very action of the brain as though it were someone else's, and to see how thoughts take their rise and then die, but it is stranger still to realize intuitively that one is about to penetrate into the mysteries which hide the innermost recesses of man's soul. I feel like some Columbus about to land on an uncharted continent. A perfectly controlled and subdued anticipation quietly thrills me.

But how to divorce oneself from the age-old tyranny of thoughts? I remember that the Maharishee has never suggested that I should attempt to force the stoppage of thinking. "Trace thought to its place of origin," is his reiterated counsel, "watch for the real self to reveal itself, and then your thoughts will die down of their own accord." So, feeling that I have found the birthplace of thinking, I let go of the powerful positive attitude which has brought my attention to this point and surrender myself to complete passivity, yet still keeping as intently watchful as a snake of its prey.

This poised condition reigns until I discover the correctness of the sage's prophecy. The waves of thought naturally begin to diminish. The workings of logical rational sense drop towards zero point. The strangest sensation I have experienced till now grips me. Time seems to reel dizzily as the antennae of my rapidly growing intuition begin to reach out into the unknown. The reports of my bodily senses are no longer heard, felt, remembered. I know that at any moment I shall be standing *outside* things, on the very edge of the world's secret . . . .

Finally it happens. Thought is extinguished like a snuffed candle. The intellect withdraws into its real ground, that is, consciousness working unhindered by thoughts. I perceive, what I have suspected for some time and what the Maharishee has confidently affirmed, that the mind takes its rise in a transcendental source. The brain has passed into a state of complete suspension, as it does in deep sleep, yet there is not the slightest loss of consciousness. I remain perfectly calm and fully aware of who I am and what is occurring. Yet my sense of awareness has been drawn out of the narrow confines of the separate personality; it has turned into something sublimely all-embracing. Self still exists, but it is a changed, radiant self. For something that is far superior to the unimportant personality which *was* I, some deeper, diviner being rises into consciousness and *becomes* me. With it arrives an amazing new sense of absolute freedom, for thought is like a loom-shuttle which is always going to and fro, and to be freed from its tyrannical motion is to step out of prison into the open air.

I find myself outside the rim of world consciousness. The planet which has so far harboured me, disappears. I am in

> the midst of an ocean of blazing light. The latter, I feel rather than think, is the primeval stuff out of which worlds are created, the first state of matter. It stretches away into untellable infinite space, incredibly *alive*.
>
> I touch, as in a flash, the meaning of this mysterious universal drama which is being enacted in space, and then return to the primal point of my being. I, the new I, rest in the lap of holy bliss. I have drunk the Platonic Cup of Lethe, so that yesterday's bitter memories and tomorrow's anxious cares have disappeared completely. I have attained a divine liberty and an almost indescribable felicity. My arms embrace all creation with profound sympathy, for I understand in the deepest possible way that to know all is not merely to pardon all, but to love all. My heart is remoulded in rapture.[199]

Paul Brunton's account, reproduced above from *A Search in Secret India*, raised the same questions in the minds of its other readers as it might well be doing in ours: is it possible to experience consciousness, without any thoughts of which one is conscious?

The question was actually put to Ramana Maharshi on March 28, 1935.

> Mrs. Ramamurthi: Swamiji, I have read Brunton's book *A Search in Secret India*, and was much impressed by the last chapter, where he says that it is possible to be conscious without thinking. I know that one can think, remaining forgetful of the physical body. Can one think without the mind? Is it possible to gain that consciousness which is beyond thoughts?
>
> M.: Yes.[200]

III
THE EXPERIENCE OF NISARGADATTA

Nisargadatta was not a disciple of Ramana though he held Ramana in high regard.[201] He attained the experience of the pure subject or the self through instructions received from his own guru. Ramana, by contrast, had no such guru.

I have selected four extracts from among many dealing with experiences of Nisargadatta with his guru and alone, which lie scattered throughout his numerous dialogues.

I

> I am now 74 years old. And yet I feel that I am an infant. I feel clearly that in spite of all the changes I am a child. My Guru told me: that child, which is you even now, is your real self ... Go back to that state of pure being, where the 'I am' is still in its purity before it got contaminated with 'this I am' or 'that I am.' Your burden is of false self-identifications—abandon them all. My Guru told me—'Trust me. I tell you; you are divine. Take it as the absolute truth. Your joy is divine, your suffering is divine too. All comes from God. Remember it always. You are God, your will alone is done.' I did believe him and soon realized how wonderfully true and accurate were his words. I did not condition my mind by thinking: 'I am God, I am wonderful, I am beyond.' I simply followed his instruction which was to focus the mind on pure being, 'I am,' and stay in it. I used to sit for hours together, with nothing but the 'I am' in my mind and soon peace and joy and a deep all-embracing love became my normal state. In it all disappeared—myself, my Guru, the life I lived, the world around me. Only peace remained and unfathomable silence.[202]

II

Questioner: Are we permitted to request you to tell us the manner of your realization?

Maharaj: Somehow it was very simple and easy in my case. My Guru, before he died, told me: Believe me, you are the Supreme Reality. Don't doubt my words, don't disbelieve me. I am telling you the truth—act on it. I could not forget his words and by not forgetting—I have realized.

Q: But what were you actually doing?

M: Nothing special. I lived my life, plied my trade, looked after my family, and every free moment I would spend just remembering my Guru and his words. He died soon after and I had only the memory to fall back on. It was enough.

Q: It must have been the grace and power of your Guru.

M: His words were true and so they came true. True words always come true. My Guru did nothing; his words acted because they were true. Whatever I did, came from within, unasked and unexpected.

Q: The Guru started a process without taking any part in it?

M: Put it as you like. Things happen as they happen—who can tell why and how? I did nothing deliberately. All came by itself—the desire to let go, to be alone, to go within.

Q: You made no efforts whatsoever?

M: None. Believe it or not, I was not even anxious to realize. He only told me that I am the Supreme and then died. I just could not disbelieve him. The rest happened by itself. I found myself changing—that is all. As a matter of fact, I was astonished. But a desire arose in me to verify his words. I was so sure that he could not possibly have told a lie, that I felt I shall either realize the full meaning of his words or die. I was feeling quite determined, but did not know what to do. I would spend hours thinking of him and his assurance, not arguing, but just remembering what he told me.

Q: What happened to you then? How did you know that you are the Supreme?

M: Nobody came to tell me. Nor was I told so inwardly. In fact, it was only in the beginning when I was making efforts, that I was passing through some strange experiences; seeing lights, hearing voices, meeting gods and goddesses and conversing with them. Once the Guru told me: 'You are the Supreme Reality,' I ceased having visions and trances and became very quiet and simple. I found myself desiring and knowing less and less, until I could say in utter astonishment: 'I know nothing, I want nothing.'

Q: Were you genuinely free of desire and knowledge, or did you impersonate a [realized being] according to the image given to you by your Guru?

M: I was not given any image, nor did I have one. My Guru never told me what to expect.

Q: More things may happen to you. Are you at the end of your journey?

M: There was never any journey. I am, as I always was.[203]

III

Q: Is the sense 'I am' real or unreal?

M: Both. It is unreal when we say: 'I am this, I am that.'

It is real when we mean 'I am not this, nor that.'

The knower comes and goes with the known, and is transient; but that which knows that it does not know, which is free of memory and anticipation, is timeless.

Q: Is 'I am' itself the witness, or are they separate?

M: Without one the other cannot be. Yet they are not one. It is like the flower and its colour. Without flower—no colours; without colour—the flower remains unseen. Beyond is the light which on contact with the flower creates the colour. Realize that your true nature is that of pure light only, and both the perceived and the perceiver come and go together. That which makes both possible, and yet is neither, is your real being, which means not being a 'this' or 'that,' but pure awareness of being and not-being. When awareness is turned on itself, the feeling is of not knowing. When it is turned outward, the knowables come into being. To say: 'I know myself' is a contradiction in terms for what is 'known' cannot be 'myself.'

Q: If the self is for ever the unknown, what then is realized in self-realization?

M: To know that the known cannot be me nor mine, is liberation enough. Freedom from self-identification with a set of memories and habits, the state of wonder at the infinite reaches of the being, its inexhaustible creativity and total transcendence, the absolute fearlessness born from the realization of the illusoriness and transiency of every mode of consciousness—flow from a deep and inexhaustible source. To know the source as source and appearance as appearance, and oneself as the source only is self-realization.

Q: On what side is the witness? Is it real or unreal?

M: Nobody can say: 'I am the witness.' The 'I am' is always witnessed. The state of detached awareness is the witness-consciousness, the 'mirror-mind.' It rises and sets with its object and thus it is not quite the real. Whatever its object, it remains the same, hence it is also real. It partakes of both the real and the unreal and is therefore a bridge between the two.

Q: If all happens only to the 'I am,' if the 'I am' is the known and the knower and the knowledge itself, what does the witness do? Of what use is it?

M: It does nothing and is of no use whatsoever.

Q: Then why do we talk of it?

M: Because it is there. The bridge serves one purpose only—to cross over. You don't build houses on a bridge. The 'I am' looks at things, the witness sees through them. It sees them as they are—unreal and transient. To say 'not me, not mine' is the talk of the witness.[204]

IV

M: And what about you? Do you shape your life or are you shaped by it?

Q: Yes, you are right. A life-story unrolls itself of which I am one of the actors. I have no being outside it, as it has no being without me. I am merely a character, not a person.

M: The character will become a person, when he begins to shape his life instead of accepting it as it comes, and identifying himself with it.

Q: When I ask a question and you answer, what exactly happens?

M: The question and the answer—both appear on the screen. The lips move, the body speaks—and again the screen is clear and empty.

Q: When you say: clear and empty, what do you mean?

M: I mean free of all contents. To myself I am neither perceivable nor conceivable; there is nothing I can point out and say: 'this I am.' You identify yourself with everything so easily; I find it impossible. The feeling: 'I am not this or that, nor is anything mine' is so strong in me that as soon as a thing or a thought appears, there comes at once the sense 'this I am not.'

Q: Do you mean to say that you spend your time repeating 'this I am not, that I am not?'

M: Of course not. I am merely verbalizing for your sake. By the grace of my Guru I have realized once and for good that I am neither object nor subject and I do not need to remind myself all the time.

Q: I find it hard to grasp what exactly do you mean by saying that you are neither the object nor the subject. At this very moment, as we talk, am I not the object of your experience, and you the subject?

M: Look, my thumb touches my forefinger. Both touch and are touched. When my attention is on the thumb, the thumb is the feeler and the forefinger—the Self. Shift the focus of attention and the relationship is reversed. I find that somehow, by shifting the focus of attention, I become the very thing I look at and experience the kind of consciousness it has; I become the inner witness of the thing. I call this capacity of entering other focal points of consciousness—love; you may give it any name you like. Love says: 'I am everything.' Wisdom says: 'I am nothing.' Between the two my life flows. Since at any point of time and space I can be both the subject and the object of experience, I express it by saying that I am both, and neither, and beyond both.

Q: You make all these extraordinary statements about yourself. What makes you say those things? What do you mean by saying that you are beyond space and time?

M: You ask and the answer comes. I watch myself—I watch the answer and see no contradiction. It is clear to me that I am telling you the truth. It is all very simple. Only you must trust me that I mean what I say, that I am quite serious. As I told you already, my Guru showed me my true nature—and the true nature of the world. Having realized that I am one with, and yet beyond the world, I became free from all desire and fear. I did not reason out that I should be free—I found myself free—unexpectedly, without the least effort. This freedom from desire and fear remained with me since then. Another thing I noticed was that I do not need to make an effort; the deed follows the thought, without delay and friction. I have also found that thoughts become self-fulfilling; things would fall in place smoothly and rightly. The main change was in the mind; it became motionless and silent, responding quickly, but not perpetuating the response. Spontaneity became a way of life, the real became natural and the natural became real. And above all, infinite affection, love, dark and quiet, radiating in all directions, embracing all, making all interesting and beautiful, significant and auspicious.[205]

CONCLUSION

The aim of this book was to present the experiential dimension of Advaita Vedanta, but that was not its purpose. Its purpose was to demonstrate that once Advaita Vedanta is presented in its experiential dimension, the draught can be distinguished from the vessel and to the extent that it was confused with the vessel, it can also be removed from it. For the natural consequence of an experiential presentation of Advaita Vedanta is to disengage it from its cultural contingencies and to unencumber it from its religious baggage. What is then left is something which we as human beings may appropriate or choose not to, depending on our judgement about it.

There is a starkness about Advaita Vedanta when presented in its experiential dimension. This starkness some find compelling and some repelling and others remain unaffected by it. All, however, would perhaps want to know: Does it have anything to offer?

The question was put to Ramana whose own virtual nakedness symbolised, as it were, the starkness of the experiential dimension of Advaita Vedanta. He was once asked by a somewhat cynical seeker: 'Do you have anything to offer to me?'

'Yes', Ramana is supposed to have said, putting aside the comic book he was reading. 'But do you think you can take it?'

NOTES

1. These cameos have been culled, in the order they appear, from: Paul Brunton, *Conscious Immortality* (Tiruvannamalai: Sri Ramanasramam, 1984) p. 177.
2. A. Devaraja Mudaliar, compiler, *Gems from Bhagavan* (Tiruvannamalai: Sri Ramanasramam, 1978) p. 56.
3. Paul Brunton, *op.cit.*, p. 85
4. Sri Nisargadatta Maharaj, *I Am That* (Bombay: Chetana, 1973) p. 477.
5. Robert Powell, ed., *The Nectar of the Lord's Feet* (Longmead: Element Books, 1987) p. 1.
6. M. Hiriyanna, *The Essentials of Indian Philosophy* (London: George Allen & Unwin, 1948) p. 22.
7. *Ibid.*, pp. 24-25.
8. *Ibid.*, p. 27
9. William M. Indich, *Consciousness in Advaita Vedanta* (Delhi: Motilal Banarsidass, 1980) p. 14.
10. T.M.P. Mahadevan, *The Insights of Advaita* (University of Mysore, 1970) p. 33.
11. David Godman, ed., *The Teachings of Sri Ramana Maharshi* (New York: Arkana, 1985) p. 37.
12. P. Sankaranarayanan, *What is Advaita*? (Bombay: Bharatiya Vidya Bhavan, 1970) p. 33.
13. Krishnachandra Bhattacharyya, "The Advaita and its Spiritual Significance" in Haridas Bhattacharyya ed., *The Cultural Heritage of India* (Calcutta: The Ramakrishna Mission Institute of Culture, 1953) Vol. III, p. 219.
14. *Ibid.*
15. William M. Indich, *op. cit.*, p. 63.
16. Sankara, as cited above.
17. K.C. Bhattacharyya, as cited above.
18. Paul Brunton, *Conscious Immortality*, p. 105.
19. *Ibid.*, p. 101.

20. Paul Brunton, *op. cit.*, p. 98: "Q. We do not know we are dreaming, whereas in waking we do?
A. The dream is a combination of waking with deep sleep. It is due to the samskaras of the waking state. Hence we remember dreams. Samskaras are not formed contrawise; hence we are not aware of the dream world simultaneously."
21. Paul Brunton, *op. cit.*, p. 100.
22. *Ibid.*, p. 103.
23. *Talks with Sri Ramana Maharshi* (Tiruvannamalai: Sri Ramanasramam, 1984) p. 375.
24. *Ibid.*, p. 101.
25. *Ibid.*, p. 98.
26. *Ibid.*, p. 104.
27. David Godman, ed., *op. cit.*, p. 16, emphasis added.
28. P. Sankaranarayanan, *op. cit.*, p. 45.
29. David Godman, ed., *op. cit.*, p. 189.
30. David Godman, ed., *op. cit.*, p. 191.
31. David Godman, ed., *op. cit.*, *p. 189.*
32. P. Sankaranarayanan, *op. cit.*, p. 46, emphasis added.
33. A. Devaraja Mudaliar, compiler, *op. cit.*, p. 36.
34. David Godman, ed., *op. cit.*, p. 189.
35. K. Satchidananda Murty, *Revelation and Reason in Advaita Vedanta* (Delhi: Motilal Banarsidass, 1974) p. 125.
36. *Talks with Sri Ramana Maharshi*, p. 564.
37. P. Sankaranarayanan, *op. cit.*, pp. 45-46.
38. Swami Rajeswarananda, compiler, *Erase the Ego* (Bombay: Bharatiya Vidya Bhavan, 1974) p. 39.
39. A. Devaraja Mudaliar, compiler, *op. cit.*, p. 5.
40. Swami Rajeswarananda, compiler, *op. cit.*, pp. 39-40.
41. William M. Indich, *op. cit.*, p. 18.
42. *Talks with Sri Ramana Maharshi*, p. 562.
43. P. Sankaranarayanan, *op. cit.*, p. 46.
44. *Talks with Sri Ramana Maharshi*, p. 469, emphasis added.
45. *Talks with Sri Ramana Maharshi*, p. 562.
46. *Ibid.*
47. William M. Indich, *op.cit.*, p. 74.
48. *Ibid.*, p. 75.
49. Paul Brunton, *op. cit.*, p. 71.
50. David Godman, ed., *op. cit.*, p. 211.
51. David Godman, ed., *op. cit.*, p. 17.
52. Swami Rajeswarananda, compiler, *op. cit.*, p. 38.
53. Quoted in P. Sankaranarayanan, *op. cit.*, p. 46.
54. *Ibid.*, p. 47.
55. Maurice Frydman, tr., *I Am That: Conversations with Sri Nisargadatta Maharaj* (Bombay: Chetana, 1973) Part I, p. 263.
56. John A. Hutchison, *Paths of Faith* (New York: McGraw-Hill Book Company, 1969) p. 222.
57. Wm. Theodore de Bary, ed., *Sources of Chinese Tradition* (New York: Columbia University Press, 1960) Vol. I., p. 73.
58. *Ibid.*, p. 72.

59. Wm. Theodore de Bary, ed., *Sources of Indian Tradition* (Delhi: Motilal Banarsidass, 1963) p. 178.
60. P. Sankaranarayanan, *op. cit.*, p. 47.
61. Swami Sambuddhananda, *Vedanta Through Stories* (Bombay: Sri Ramakrishna Ashram, 1959) pp. 44-45.
62. A. Devaraja Mudaliar, compiler, *op. cit.*, pp. 24-25, parenthetical material added.
63. *Talks with Ramana Maharshi*, pp. 466-67.
64. T.M.P. Mahadevan, *The Insights of Advaita* (University of Mysore, 1970) p. 33.
65. David Godman, ed., *op. cit.*, p. 11.
66. *Talks with Sri Ramana Maharshi*, p. 468.
67. David Godman, ed., *op. cit.*, p. 14.
68. M. Hiriyanna, *Essentials of Indian Philosophy*, p. 166.
69. *Ibid.*
70. Paul Brunton, *op. cit.*, pp. 113-14.
71. Swami Rajeswarananda, compiler, *op. cit.*, p. 26.
72. *Ibid.*, pp. 40-41, emphasis added.
73. See William M. Indich, *op. cit.*, p. 37.
74. David Godman, ed., *op. cit.*, p. 26.
75. "This phenomenological analysis of the deep sleep state is extremely important for the Advaitin, for it is in terms of this analysis that he argues for the non-dual, self-luminous and, as we have seen in a previous chapter, the blissful nature of pure consciousness. It may seem somewhat odd to a person trained in Western philosophy that an analysis of dreamless sleep should play a significant role in the philosophical defense of a particular theory of consciousness. Of course, both Freud and Jung saw in sleep a physiologically and psychologically necessary period of relief and recovery from the strains of waking experience, a point that goes back at least as far as Aristotle, but there seems to be little of philosophical concern for these thinkers behind this observation. On the other hand, while Sankara discusses the physiology of sleep and acknowledges its value in allowing the individual to recover from fatigue, he goes beyond this and extracts arguments for his theory of Self from his discussion of sleep. And he is not alone among Indian philosophers in doing this." (William M. Indich, *op. cit.*, p. 97).
76. *Talks with Sri Ramana Maharshi*, p. 563.
77. *Ibid.*
78. William M. Indich, *op. cit.*, p. 65.
79. William M. Indich, *op. cit.*, p. 37.
80. Paul Brunton, *op. cit.*, p. 127.
81. Paul Brunton, *op. cit.*, p. 184.
82. M. Hiriyanna, *The Essentials of Indian Philosophy*, p. 166.
83. Paul Brunton, *op. cit.*, p. 116.
84. A. Devaraja Mudaliar, compiler, *op. cit.*, p. 35.
85. Paul Brunton, *op. cit.*, p. 91.
86. David Godman, ed., *op. cit.*, p. 53.
87. David Godman, ed., *op. cit.*, p. 52.
88. *Ibid.*
89. Swami Rajeswarananda, compiler, *op. cit.*, p. 39.

90. A. Devaraja Mudaliar, compiler, *op. cit.*, p. 17.
91. Swami Rajeswarananda, çompiler, *op. cit.*, p. 55.
92. Arthur Osborne, ed., *op. cit.*, p. 249.
93. *Ibid.*, p. 228.
94. T.M.P. Mahadevan, tr., *Who Am I?* (Tiruvannamalai: Sri Ramanasramam, 1976) p. 2.
95. David Godman, ed., *op. cit.*, p. 50.
96. *Ibid.*, p. 52.
97. *Ibid.*, p. 14.
98. M. Hiriyanna, *The Essentials of Indian Philosophy*, p. 65.
99. Paul Brunton, *op. cit.*, p. 160.
100. David Godman, ed., *op. cit.*, p. 37.
101. Arthur Osborne, ed. *op. cit.*, p. 238.
102. *Ibid.*, p. 244.
103. David Godman, ed., *op. cit.*, p. 40.
104. *Ibid.*, p. 41.
105. David Godman, ed., *op. cit.*, p. 211. 'Realized being' is *jnani* in the original.
106. *Ibid.*, p. 208.
107. *Ibid.*, p. 212.
108. *Ibid.*
109. B.V. Narasimha Swami, *Self Realization: The Life and Teachings of Sri Ramana Maharshi* (Tiruvannamalai: Sri Ramanasramam, 1985) p. 103.
110. David Godman, ed., *op. cit.*, p. 41.
111. Maurice Frydman, tr., *op. cit.* p. 117.
112. David Godman, ed., *op. cit.*, p. 37.
113. *Ibid.*, p. 38.
114. Arthur Osborne, ed., *op. cit.*, p. 248.
115. David Godman, ed., *op. cit.*, p. 36.
116. *Ibid.*, p. 42.
117. *Ibid.*, p. 41.
118. Paul Brunton, *op. cit.*, p. 166.
119. *Ibid.*,
120. *Ibid.*,
121. *Ibid.*, p. 101.
122. Maurice Frydman, tr., *op. cit.*, p. 410.
123. Arthur Osborne, ed., *op. cit.*, p. 246.
124. *Ibid.*, p. 210.
125. *Ibid.*, p. 192.
126. Jadunath Sinha, *A History of Indian Philosophy* (Calcutta: Sinha Publishing House, 1956) p. 286.
127. T.M.P. Mahadevan, *Gaudapada: A Study in Early Advaita* (University of Madras, 1960) p. 100.
128. William M. Indich, *op. cit.*, p. 53.
129. Bhagwan Shree Rajneesh, *op. cit.*, pp. 179-80.
130. Edward Conze, *Buddhism: Its Essence and Development* (New York: Harper & Row, 1959) p. 101.
131. *Ibid.*, p. 198.
132. M. Hiriyanna, *Outlines of Indian Philosophy* (Bombay: Blackie & Son, 1983) pp. 192-93. The citation constitutes a single unit in the original.
133. William M. Indich, *op. cit.*, p. 18.

134. Edward Conze, *op. cit.*, p. 167.
135. Edward Conze writes (*op. cit.*, p. 166): "The subject is identified by the Abhidharma with the skandha of Consciousness, defined by *Awareness* as its essential mark. Just as the blade of a knife cannot cut itself, so we cannot experience consciousness directly, as an object in front of us. For as soon as we turn to the subject, it becomes an object and ceases to be the subject. Introspection can thus never hope to meet the subject face to face. The final subject—which might be at the end of the infinite regress—is completely beyond our experience, it is not really of this world, it is transcendental. To try to get to it would be to attempt the impossible." Perhaps, but not according to Advaita!
136. A.L. Basham, *The Wonder That was India* (New York: Grove Press Inc., 1954) p. 271.
137. M. Hiriyanna, *Essentials of Indian Philosophy*, p. 79.
138. M. Hiriyanna, *Outlines of Indian Philosophy*, p. 145.
139. *Ibid.*,
140. G.P. Malalasekera, ed., *Encyclopedia of Buddhism* (Government of Ceylon, 1961) Vol. I, p. 571.
141. Walpola Sri Rahula, *What the Buddha Taught* (New York: Grove Press, Inc., 1974) Chapter VI.
142. *Ibid.*, also see G.P. Malalasekera, ed., *op. cit.*, pp. 573ff; Edward Conze, *op. cit.*, pp. 168ff.
143. Walpola Sri Rahula, *op. cit.*, p. 56.
144. William M. Indich, *op. cit.*, pp. 34-35.
145. Edward Conze, *op. cit.*, p. 169.
146. David Godman, ed., *op. cit.*, p. 64. Also see pp. 34, 53, 210 etc.
147. Swami Rajeswarananda, compiler, p. 37.
148. Paul Brunton, *op. cit.*, p. 77.
149. Swami Rajeswarananda, compiler, *op. cit.*, p. 14.
150. A. Devaraja Mudaliar, *op. cit.*, p. 38, emphasis added.
151. *Talks with Sri Ramana Maharshi*, p. 56.
152. William M. Indich, *op. cit.*, p. 34.
153. *Talks with Sri Ramana Maharshi*, p. 5. For the use of the same expression in the context of the ultimate state of Yoga see M. Hiriyanna, *The Essentials of Indian Philosophy*, p. 124.
154. *Talks with Sri Ramana Maharshi*, p. 23.
155. *Ibid.*, p. 52, emphasis added.
156. Paul Brunton, *op. cit.*, p. 7.
157. *Ibid.*, p. 101, emphasis added.
158. *Ibid.*, p. 103.
159. William M. Indich, *op. cit.*, p. 65.
160. *Talks with Sri Ramana Maharshi*, p. 563.
161. Ann Faraday, *Dream Power* (New York: Berkeley Books, 1980) p. 96.
162. *Ibid.*, pp. 93-94.
163. *Ibid.*, p. 38.
164. Swami Sri Ramanananda Saraswathi, tr., *Tripura Rahasya or the Mystery Beyond the Trinity* (Tiruvannamalai: Sri Ramanasramam, 1980) p. 155.
165. *Ibid.*
166. *Ibid.*, p. 156. However it could be argued that incontradictability or undeniability *is* proof of reality: "*Reality must endure for ever and ever.*

'Consciousness either *is* or *is not*.' In the former case, it is obvious and in the latter it is implied, for the conception of its absence implies consciousness. (Therefore consciousness cannot be established to be transitory. It is permanent and therefore real.)

Insentient matter is diverse in nature and its impermanency obvious. For, one object excludes all others.

But can you conceive the absence of consciousness anywhere or at any time? If you say that there is no awareness in your sleep, tell me how you know that period or again how you know that you were not aware. If absolutely unaware, you would not now be able to say—'I was not aware.' How was this unawareness illumined for you? Therefore you cannot escape the conclusion that there must be consciousness even to know its unawareness also. So, there is no moment when consciousness is not." (*Ibid.*, pp. 155-56).

167. Satischandra Chatterjee and Dhirendramohan Datta, *An Introduction to Indian Philosophy* (University of Calcutta, 1950) p. 393.
168. *Ibid.*, p. 387.
169. T.M.P. Mahadevan, *Gaudapada: A Study in Early Advaita* (University of Madras, 1960) p. 127.
170. Ann Farady, *op. cit.*, pp. 26, 30, 52, 70, 77, 81, 82, 87, 102, 218.
171. *Ibid.*, pp. 21, 24.
172. *Ibid.*, p. 298.
173. *Ibid.*, p. 303.
174. Paul Brunton, *op. cit.*, p. 86, emphasis added.
175. Paul Brunton, *op. cit.*, p. 97.
176. David Godman, ed., *The Teachings of Sri Ramana Maharshi* (New York: Arkana, 1985) p. 69.
177. Swami Rajeswarananda, compiler, *op. cit.*, p. 20.
178. Paul Brunton, *op. cit.*, p. 68.
179. David Godman, ed., *The Teachings of Sri Ramana Maharshi* (New York: Arkana, 1985) p. 56.
180. *Talks with Sri Ramana Maharshi*, p. 307.
181. Swami Rajeswarananda, compiler, *op. cit.*, p. 24.
182. Swami Rajeswarananda, compiler, *op. cit.*, p. 18.
183. Paul Brunton, *op. cit.*, p. 102.
184. *Ibid.*, p. 104.
185. A. Devaraja Mudaliar, *op. cit.*, p. 25.
186. Swami Rajeswarananda, compiler, *op. cit.*, p. 29.
187 *Talks with Sri Ramana Maharshi*, p. 13.
188. Swami Sri Ramananda Saraswathi, tr., *op. cit.*, pp. 68, 121.
189. David Godman, ed., *op. cit.*, p. 49.
190. *Ibid.*, p. 59.
191. *Ibid.*, pp. 57-58.
192. David Godman, ed., *op. cit.*, p. 57; Arthur Osborne, ed., *op. cit.*, Chapter 3, etc.
193. Paul Brunton, *Conscious Immortality* , pp. 130-31.
194. B.V. Narasimha Swami, *Self-Realization: The Life and Teaching of Sri Ramana Maharshi* (Tiruvannamalai: Sri Ramanasramam, 1985; first published 1931) p. 20.
195. *Ibid.*, pp. 20-22

196. Paul Brunton, *op. cit.*, p. 68.
197. B.V. Narasimha Swami, *op. cit.*, p. 231.
198. Paul Brunton, *A Search in Secret India* (New York: E.P. Dutton & Co., Inc., 1952; first published 1935).
199. *Ibid.*, pp. 301-305.
200. *Talks with Sri Ramana Maharshi*, p. 49.
201. Maurice Frydman, tr., *op. cit.*, p. 157.
202. *Ibid.*, p. 239.
203. *Ibid.*, pp. 391-92.
204. *Ibid.*, pp. 395-96.
205. *Ibid.*, pp. 268-69.

BIBLIOGRAPHY

Wm. Theodore de Bary, ed. *Sources of Indian Tradition*. Delhi: Motilal Banarsidass, 1963.

________ , ed. *Sources of Chinese Tradition*. New York: Columbia University Press, 1960.

A.L. Basham. *The Wonder That was India*. New York: Grove Press Inc., 1954.

Haridas Bhattacharyya, ed. *The Cultural Heritage of India*. Calcutta: The Ramakrishna Mission Institute of Culture, 1953.

Paul Brunton. *Conscious Immortality*. Tiruvannamalai: Sri Ramanasramam, 1984.

________ . *A Search in Secret India*. New York: E.P. Dutton & Co., Inc., 1952; first published 1935.

Satischandra Chatterjee and Dhirendramohan Datta. *An Introduction to Indian Philosophy*. Calcutta: University of Calcutta, 1950.

Edward Conze. *Buddhism: Its Essence and Development*. New York: Harper & Row, 1959.

Maurice Frydman, tr. *I am That: Conversations with Sri Nisargadatta Maharaj*. Bombay: Chetana, 1973.

David Godman, ed. *The Teachings of Sri Ramana Maharshi*. New York: Arkana, 1985.

M. Hiriyanna. *Outlines of Indian Philosophy*. Bombay: Blackie & Son, 1983.

________ . *The Essentials of Indian Philosophy*. London: Allen & Unwin, 1948.

John A. Hutchinson. *Paths of Faith*. New York: McGraw-Hill Book Company, 1969.

William M. Indich. *Consciousness in Advaita Vedanta*. Delhi: Motilal Banarsidass, 1980.

T.M.P. Mahadevan, tr. *Who Am I?* Tiruvannamalai: Sri Ramanasramam, 1976.

________ . *The Insights of Advaita*. Mysore: University of Mysore, 1970.

________. *Gaudapada: A Study of Early Advaita*. Madras: University of Madras, 1960.

G.P. Malalasekera, ed. *Encyclopedia of Buddhism*. Ceylon: Government of Ceylon. 1961.

A. Devaraja Mudaliar, compiler, *Gems from Bhagavan*. Tiruvannamalai: Sri Ramanasramam, 1978.

K. Satchidananda Murty. *Revelation and Reason in Advaita Vedanta*. Delhi: Motilal Banarsidass, 1974.

Robert Powell, ed. *The Nectar of the Lord's Feet*. Longmead: Element Books, 1987.

Walpola Sri Rahula. *What the Buddha Taught*. New York: Grove Press, Inc., 1974.

Swami Rajeswarananda, compiler. *Erase the Ego*. Bombay: Bharatiya Vidya Bhavan, 1974.

Swami Sambuddhananda. *Vedanta Through Stories*. Bombay: Sri Ramakrishna Ashram, 1959.

P. Sankaranarayanan. *What is Advaita*? Bombay: Bharatiya Vidya Bhavan, 1974.

Swami Sri Ramanananda Saraswathi, tr. *Tripura Rahasya or the Mystery Beyond the Trinity*. Tiruvannamalai: Sri Ramanasramam, 1980.

Jadunath Sinha. *A History of Indian Philosophy*. Calcutta: Sinha Publishing House, 1956.

B.V. Narasimha Swami. *Self-Realization: The Life and Teaching of Sri Ramana Maharshi*. Tiruvannamalai: Sri Ramanasramam, 1985; first published 1931.

Talks with Sri Ramana Maharshi. Tiruvannamalai: Sri Ramanasramam, 1984.

GLOSSARY

ADVAITA VEDANTA: That school of Hindu philosophy according to which the final teaching of the *Upanisads*, the *Brahmamutra* and the *Bhagavadgita* is non-dualism, viz. that Brahman, which is identical with Atman, is the sole ultimate reality.

AVASTHA-TRAYA: The doctrine that all normal human experience is comprised within 'three states', namely, those of waking (*jagrata*), dreaming (*svapna*) and deep sleep (*susupti*), with the additional implication that it is also possible to realize a fourth (*turiya*) state of mystical experience.

NISARGADATTA MAHARAJ (1897-1981): An Advaitin whose reputation as an experiential exponent of Advaita is rapidly spreading through his numerous dialogues published under the title: *I Am That*.

RAMANA MAHARSHI (1879-1950): The foremost experiential exponent of the school of Advaita Vedanta in modern times, who has been hailed by T.M.P. Mahadevan, not without a touch of paradox, as "an incarnation of pure Advaita".

SANKARA OR SANKARACARYA (Circa 788-820 C.E.): The foremost exponent of the school of Hindu philosophy known as Advaita Vedanta.

INDEX